THE
McGRAW-HILL
36-Hour Course

LEAN
SIX SIGMA

Sheila Shaffie
Shahbaz Shahbazi

Mc
Graw
Hill

New York   Chicago   San Francisco   Lisbon   London
Madrid   Mexico City   Milan   New Delhi   San Juan
Seoul   Singapore   Sydney   Toronto

1 2 3 4 5 6 7 8 9 10   QFR/QFR   1 8 7 6 5 4 3 2

ISBN   978-0-07-174385-3
MHID   0-07-174385-5

e-ISBN   978-0-07-175085-1
e-MHID   0-07-175085-1

Library of Congress Cataloging-in-Publication Data

Shaffie, Sheila.
    The McGraw-Hill 36-hour course : lean six sigma / Sheila Shaffie and Shahbaz Shahbazi.
       p. cm.—(McGraw-Hill 36-hour courses)
    ISBN 978-0-07-174385-3 (pbk.)—ISBN 0-07-174385-5 ()
    1. Six sigma (Quality control standard) 2. Total quality management.
   3. Organizational effectiveness.
   4. Quality control.   I. Shahbazi, Shahbaz.   II. Title.   III. Title: McGraw-Hill thirty-six hour course.

   HD62.15.S475 2012
     658.4'013—dc23   2012000522

Portions of information contained in this publication/book are printed with permission of Minitab Inc. All such material remains the exclusive property and copyright of Minitab Inc. All rights reserved.

This book is printed on acid-free paper.

CONTENTS

INTRODUCTION

With the integration of the Lean and Six Sigma methodologies—the Big Bang of the quality movement—the business world finally has at its disposal the tools it needs to actually deliver top-quality service and products. As we shall see in this book, it is up to the leaders of each organization to make the tough decisions and transform their organization from one that uses catchphrases and sexy slogans to attract customers (only to lose them a few months later) to one that actually has the facts and data to back up the claims it makes about being a "quality organization." The truth is that the GDP of the United States has seen a steady shift from manufacturing to services over the last two decades, and the visible differentiation in the nonmanufacturing sector is through service delivery and product ingenuity. Lean Six Sigma is based on the premise that in order to deliver service and product excellence, firms must not only have an in-depth knowledge of their internal processes, but also have a profound understanding of customers' current expectations and future needs.

1

While they are still two distinct practices and philosophies, the integration of Lean and Six Sigma has created an approach that is more flexible and applicable when addressing business challenges. Lean Six Sigma helps companies make the transformation from a more traditional business and operational management model to a process management one. This transformation allows for increased clarity, consistency, ownership, and control of business processes.

This book aims to introduce you to Lean Six Sigma and to help you make informed decisions about this methodology. Our learning objectives for you are to enable you to:

- Understand why a company should utilize the Six Sigma and Lean methodologies
- Learn the roles of measurement and statistics in Six Sigma
- Gain exposure to a range of tools, from simple to advanced
- Understand the value of combining Six Sigma with Lean methodology
- Understand when and why to apply Six Sigma and Lean tools
- Engage in a step-by-step application of the methodology and tools
- Develop a rollout plan and outline the roles of executives and leaders in supporting that plan

BUILDING THE CASE FOR QUALITY

There are several reasons why an organization needs to establish a quality culture.

Letting the Numbers Tell the Story

While this is less often lacking in organizations today, the need for quality must be established within an organization well before the organization sets out on this journey. Every company will have its own set of objectives; however, a study by Hendricks and Singhal, titled *Empirical Evidence from Firms That Have Won Quality Awards*, clearly showed that the bottom-line performance of companies that emphasize quality is markedly improved. This study was an empirical review of all Quality Award winners over a 10-year period. According to the study's findings, the award-winning companies experienced:

- A 91 percent growth in operating revenue compared to 43 percent for the control group
- A 69 percent increase in sales compared to 32 percent
- A 79 percent increase in total assets compared to 37 percent
- A 23 percent increase in number of employees compared to 7 percent
- An 8 percent rise in return on sales compared to no improvement for the control group
- A 9 percent improvement in return on assets compared to 6 percent

Looking at these data, we can safely say that effective implementation of quality principles leads to an improvement in long-term financial performance for most organizations.

Fundamentally, organizations deploy Lean Six Sigma to help alleviate market pressures and, in the process, to transform themselves into more responsive and competitive entities. To achieve the types of results observed in the Hendricks and Singhal study, an organization has to set out on a quality journey. Lean Six Sigma can help an organization achieve quantifiable improvements by:

- Creating a sustainable quality culture
  - Bringing clarity to "invisible" processes and enhancing control

- Providing a corporate strategy for differentiation
  - Becoming a world-class service or product provider at the lowest cost
  - Providing customers with what *they* value
  - Reducing the hidden costs associated with poor-quality products or services
- Disproving the perception that Lean Six Sigma applies only in manufacturing

Building a Sustainable Quality Culture

Since the 1980s, organizations have attempted to introduce quality methodologies with varying degrees of success. The reasons for their success or failure are numerous, but one reason stands out more than any other: the lack of a sustainable quality culture. With Lean Six Sigma (LSS), an organization is setting out on a distinct journey using common operating mechanisms, training, an organizational structure, objectives, and a common language. The fact that LSS is increasingly the approach to quality chosen by both large and small organizations is in large part because it has staying power; it is a proven methodology that has produced measurable financial results over two decades. If an organization and all its various divisions have accepted the introduction of LSS, they are all working toward a common strategic goal, and they all understand the path to attaining this goal, then the effectiveness of LSS is greatly enhanced.

One way in which LSS helps in the development of a sustainable quality culture is by assessing business process performance in an unbiased fashion. Outside of the manufacturing world, where we can see the product that is being created and visually inspect it for defects, controling quality becomes more difficult. How do we inspect our product throughout its development if it is a loan, an insurance policy, or the transfer of patient records from a hospital to a clinic? The truth is that most of these products and processes are invisible, meaning that we rely on a transfer of information to complete the task and deliver the product or service. And it is increasingly difficult to conduct quality control on information transfer; we must have a mechanism in place to notify us that, for example, file transfer between the branch and the back office has slowed drastically, with the result that customers are being made to wait an extra 10 days to open an account. Simple Lean Six Sigma tools like value stream mapping and process maps can bring to light things that have been assumed or are not well understood. By making what resides inside people's heads or systems (invisible) visible on a map, an organization can not only identify opportunities for improvement, but create a baseline for current performance.

There are two further points that emphasize LSS's strength in promoting sustainability:

1. LSS projects are typically linked to business-critical issues. This ensures that the LSS teams are assigned to address challenging issues and deliver quantifiable benefits, and that they get the level of attention and support required for long-term success.

2. LSS provides a standard approach to problem solving. Management and executives can be sure that the appropriate level of rigor has been applied and that the team has worked to find the root cause. In short, LSS stops employees from jumping from problem statement to solution.

DEVELOPING A CORPORATE STRATEGY FOR DIFFERENTIATION

The LSS methodology helps an organization successfully make the transition to one that differentiates itself by:

1. Offering top-level service
2. Simultaneously offering products or services that the customer values
3. Having the lowest level of operating expenses

This transformation takes place because the organization better understands the needs and wants of its customer base, is able to measure and monitor its vendors' performance, and improves its internal business processes. It is undeniable that the degree of difference between the products or services of competitors is shrinking. How do customers differentiate between companies when the products being offered are basically the same? How does a car buyer choose between lenders when deciding on a loan provider? The rates are almost identical. The answer to this question is the foundation of quality in an organization, from both a product and a service delivery dimension. The more we understand what the end buyers want and how we perform to their expectations, the clearer the road map for improvement will be. This is how Lean Six Sigma is being utilized in the marketplace today to create differentiation.

HELPING TO OVERCOME OPERATIONAL CHALLENGES

Regardless of an organization's industry or size, there are three types of challenges that can prevent it from operating effectively, leaving it with inefficient processes and poor service delivery. These challenges are:

1. Introducing new processes or products without:
   - Having a complete understanding of risk, that is, recognizing what could go wrong, how to address it, and its impact on other parts of the organization
   - Success metrics—how to know if the goals have been reached
2. One-at-a-time changes or improvements—being in reactive mode:
   - Adversely affecting one process while trying to fix another
   - Not allowing for a cohesive, strategic fix
3. Lack of appropriate in-process and executive metrics:
   - Not knowing what to measure, how to measure it, and how often
   - Failing to drive continuous improvement based on employee noise level

These challenges arise because organizations don't have a systematic problem-solving platform or a business culture that is based on process management and data-driven decision making. Regardless of the type of challenge facing the organization, the fact remains that executives need a systematic and structured approach to dealing with business issues. Most often, this structured approach comes directly from the quality strategy that has been implemented. The strengths of Lean Six Sigma are that it helps organizations overcome these challenges by providing a common language, training, and a problem-solving tool kit. It will help ensure that all business decisions, whether they involve buying a new core system or launching a new product, are based on data (customer, market, process capability, and so on). From a process improvement perspective, it ensures that the process is being looked at holistically, taking into consideration its natural start and end points, and thus mitigating the risk of reengineering only a piece of the process and having an adverse impact on other parts of the organization.

GOALS AND SUCCESS METRICS OF LEAN SIX SIGMA

Any meaningful initiative needs to have success metrics. Organizations need to continuously gauge the effectiveness of their Lean Six Sigma deployment. The four main goals of a LSS deployment are:

1. Reduce operational cost and risk
   - Increase efficiency and predictability
   - Reduce the cost associated with poor quality
2. Increase revenue
   - Reduce leakage
3. Improve customer service—deliver consistent customer service
4. Build a culture of continuous improvement

Reduce Operational Cost and Risk

For most companies operating today, operational cost and risk are significant factors contributing to lower profits, or even losses. While some risk cannot be eliminated and operational cost is ubiquitous, Lean Six Sigma can provide a road map that can drastically reduce an organization's exposure to risk while making the organization more efficient at delivering its product or service. An example of a cost-reduction project would be a focus on decreasing process cycle time. The end result will be a streamlined process with fewer touchpoints, fewer non-value-adding activities, less rework, and fewer failures, all of which will reduce cost. Additional benefits may be consistently meeting service-level agreements (SLAs) with customers, avoiding penalties, and recognizing revenue faster. Another main focal area for Lean Six Sigma is projects to reduce cost associated with poor quality. For companies that choose to ignore the importance of quality in their operations and their product offering, it is important to outline the impact that this will have on their bottom line. On average, U.S. companies dedicate about 15 percent of their sales to resolving quality matters. For our purposes here, I will point out some of the more blatant tangible and intangible costs associated with providing products or services with poor quality.

Tangible Costs

Inspection. Anytime we have to inspect a service or product, we are performing a step that our customers do *not* want to pay for. In the ideal (Lean Six Sigma) world, the product or service would never arrive at a particular point in a deficient or incomplete form. The flow or process would be set up in such a way that any potential errors will be captured and fixed at the process step where they occur.

Process waste. This includes any activity that adds cost or time to the process but does not change the fit, form, or function of the product or service being delivered. Examples are scanning, mail distribution, and rechecking.

Rework. This implies redoing something that has ostensibly already been done. Without any doubt, we can say that no customer wants to bear this cost. The idea of rework implies that the process has been set up in a way that allows incomplete or incorrect work to pass further along in the process, so that it must be caught (and corrected) by someone downstream.

Complaints. If we can minimize the reasons for a customer complaint, we will reduce cost to the organization. Complaints can affect our bottom line drastically in cases where the product or service has some critical faults. Also, complaints can lead to the loss of repeat business from an existing client.

Intangible Costs

These are costs associated with our failures in the quality realm that are hard to quantify. For example, losing customers has multiple effects on an organization. A lost customer will inform several other people of his experience, in addition to causing the company decreased revenue. Managing angry customers and handling complaints are also examples of intangible costs that should be reduced using LSS.

Increase Revenue

Opportunities for increasing revenue can be uncovered by a better understanding of customer needs and wants, and also by identification of leakage points. Typical Lean Six Sigma projects on the revenue side focus on improving cross-selling activities (increasing the products per customer ratio), improving the repurchase rate for similar goods or services, or increasing application conversion rates. With regard to conversion rates, think of the number of applications that a bank or credit union may receive for car loans—how many of those applications are actually converted into loans? The goal of a Lean Six Sigma project would be to recognize the major dropout points or leakage points in the process and identify ways to reduce or eliminate them. Ultimately the goal is to improve the company's bottom line.

Deliver Consistent Customer Service

The image of your company is created in large part by its interaction with customers. You want this interaction to be as consistent as possible because disappointed customers are vocal critics. Lean Six Sigma can help identify the amount of variation your customers are experiencing, what is driving that variation, and ultimately, how the number of dissatisfied customers can be minimized.

Build a Culture of Continuous Improvement

No methodology will have staying power if it does not instill a single-minded focus on continuous improvement within employees. Lean Six Sigma is built on a platform that constantly revisits the idea of improving processes and customer impact. If the central focus of an organization is on continuous improvement, chances are that in the long term, that organization will not be in reactive mode. The role of Lean Six Sigma in building a continuous improvement culture is significant, including:

- A standard approach to problem solving
- A common language, organizational structure (Green Belts, Black Belts, and so on), and culture for measuring business process performance
- The creation of infrastructure in the company to permit access to reliable and timely process data so that accurate business decisions can be made
- The development of meaningful process metrics that help gauge performance as well as identify future improvement opportunities

THE IMPORTANCE OF LSS IN NONMANUFACTURING SECTORS

At some point in this discussion, we have to consider why this methodology should be embraced by nonmanufacturing companies that are hoping to deliver better service and product to their customers.

None of these should come as a surprise, given the volume of information about the application of LSS to the services, healthcare, and financial sectors.

Up to 50 Percent of Service Cost Is Non-Value-Added Work in Your Customers' Eyes

In other words, about 50 percent of the costs associated with delivering service are for things that customers do *not* want to pay for. The need to reexamine an application for completeness, the need to double-check whether an amount is correct, and the need to verify an account type are all activities that customers consider unnecessary, as they expect the work to have been done correctly the first time.

Much Service Work Is Invisible, and Invisible Work Is Hard to Improve

One of the truisms for the service sector (and increasingly for the U.S. economy as a whole) is the fact that the work being performed is not visible. We work on data entry, make judgments on applications, and respond to customer requests online. These are all activities that do not involve visual observation of a product. We are manipulating information and data on a customer application, not observing the manufacture of a mobile phone. It is easier to identify defects when we can observe a cellular phone as it goes through manufacturing than when we process an application for a home mortgage. In the case of the mortgage, once the applicant triggers the request, the information enters a pipeline and must pass through several different silos within the organization before a response is delivered to the customer. Most often, there is minimal communication between these silos, and for this reason an application can easily get held up (for example, at underwriting). Unless the work environment can be made visible, either by process mapping or by the development of daily process metrics, it is difficult to identify improvement or risk-reduction opportunities.

We Add Value to the End Product or Service Only 5 to 10 Percent of the Time

Let's take the example of applying for a new health insurance policy and look at the totality of the effort required to process that application before a policy is issued to the customer. In reality, while that application is in our possession, we are adding value 5 to 10 percent of the time. The other 90 to 95 percent of the time is considered waste; it includes such things as checking, rechecking, waiting for information, waiting for approval, and reentering information, and all these activities add no value to the final product. It is for our internal purposes (regulatory and compliance) or because of our internal process structure (system limitation, organizational structure, or poor process design) that we have this inefficiency and redundancy.

The 80/20 Rule Holds True

There have always been delays in the service sector—this is a fact of life, and we have gotten used to it. These can include waiting for a debit card to arrive or a business owner's line-of-credit renewal getting caught up in the paper shuffle. But in reality, these delays don't have to be as pervasive a problem as we currently observe. The fact is that more than 80 percent of delays are caused by less than 20 percent of activities. For those of us in the quality realm, this means that by tackling a small segment of business processes, we can achieve far-reaching improvements.

The reality is that competition is fierce and customers are more informed. The combination of these two factors is leading to a decrease in your customers' loyalty. To stay ahead of the game, forward-thinking businesses will challenge their staff members and force them to make tough decisions based on data, not on intuition or gut instinct. LSS provides a platform that allows organizations to combat this negative environment; it encourages an organization to listen to its customers' demands and then use that information to change for the better.

DEFINING SIX SIGMA, LEAN, AND LEAN SIX SIGMA

Before we look at implementation, we should first define the terms we are using and take a brief look at the history of these methodologies.

Six Sigma

In the late 1970s, many U.S.-based companies began adopting quality initiatives. In many cases, they started down this path because their backs were up against the wall. Leading manufacturers were losing market share to overseas competitors, particularly those from Japan. At that time, Japanese companies were using Total Quality Control (TQC) and Lean principles to improve manufacturing performance and to design "customer-centric" products. In response, U.S. firms began adopting Total Quality Management (TQM), a variation of TQC. In the 1990s, Jack Welch, the CEO of General Electric, began touting the benefits of a new quality game changer: Six Sigma. The world of quality began to converge on Six Sigma because of the benefits it delivered and its flexibility in terms of being able to apply it to any functional business area. Today, it has made its way through all the major segments of the U.S. economy: financial services, healthcare, defense, government, and manufacturing. Six Sigma is a statistical problem-solving methodology and a management philosophy, one that dictates that business and process decisions should be based on data. It contains five distinct problem-solving phases known as the DMAIC approach:

- *Define* the problem statement, the goal, and the financial benefits.
- *Measure* the current performance of the process and collect the required data.
- *Analyze* the root cause of the problem.
- *Improve* the process to eliminate errors and instability.
- *Control* the performance of the process, ensuring that the improvements are sustained.

Six Sigma's fundamental goal is to reduce operational variance by improving the overall quality and performance levels of business processes. This is particularly critical in the service sector, as customers are more likely to take notice of service variance, or "foul-ups."

Unfortunately, most customers don't remember an organization's general performance over time. Statistically, attaining Six Sigma implies having processes that produce only 3.4 defects per million opportunities. Therefore, if a bank provides one million loans, only 3.4 of them are closed with errors. Figure I.1 outlines the relationship

Figure I.1   Sigma Level, Accuracy, and Number of Defects

	Sigma Level	% Accuracy	Number of Defects per Million Opportunities
Excellence ↓	2	69%	308,537
	3	93%	66,807
	4	99.4%	6,210
	5	99.97%	233
	6	99.9997%	3.4

between a sigma score, the accuracy of the process (the probability of getting the transaction done right the first time), and the number of defects if there were 1 million of those transactions.

As the process capability increases, so does the sigma value, indicating that there is a lower probability of making a mistake. While achieving Six Sigma is a desirable goal, only a few industries, such as the pharmaceutical and airline industries, need to attain these accuracy levels in their processes.

In most sectors, a four sigma level (99.379 percent accuracy) is a highly noteworthy accomplishment. Furthermore, it is commonly accepted today that embarking on the "quality journey" is in itself an important step. As mentioned earlier, customers are more apt to take issue with situations in which things don't proceed the way they have come to expect.

The strength of Six Sigma is based on its quality culture infrastructure. This methodology has well-defined roles and responsibilities, such as Green Belts, Black Belts, and Master Black Belts; training; language; and a particular(read data-driven) mindset. In a nutshell, Six Sigma is a problem-solving methodology that uses human assets, data, measurements, and statistics to eliminate waste and defects while increasing customer satisfaction, profit, and customer value. If it is implemented correctly, the key deliverables are:

- **Improved service reliability**—consistency of performance and delivering the service right the first time.
- **Improved responsiveness**—timeliness of the response and readiness to provide the service when the customer wants it.
- **Improved assurance**—creating trust and confidence in the customer base.
- **Reduced expenses**—improving the effectiveness and accuracy of business processes.

- **Increased revenue**—understanding what your customers want, when they want it, and what is the right price.

The hidden cost of variation—defects and waste—can total in the millions of dollars. This variation often comes from not having access to information. The Six Sigma methodology helps organizations identify what they don't know *and* emphasizes what they should know. It then provides a road map for taking corrective action to reduce the errors and rework that ultimately cost the organization money, opportunities, and customers. Robust processes—those that produce low error rates—have a direct impact on overall productivity, customer satisfaction, and profitability.

Lean

Lean is a philosophy that is focused on shortening the timeline between the customer request and the delivery of the service by eliminating waste. This ensures that every activity and process step adds *value* to the end product or service. Lean methodology defines waste as any activity that adds time and cost but does not improve the fit, form, or function of the service or product that is delivered to the customer. There are seven types of waste, as outlined in Table I.1.

The creation of perfect value for the customer is Lean's core objective. However, to attain this, an organization needs to:

- Understand customers' needs and wants
- Identify key waste elements that affect the performance and quality of the service or product

Knowing both your customers' needs and the areas of waste within your organization allows you to create processes that deliver

Table I.1 The Seven Types of Waste

Type of Waste	Description
Defects	Any nonconformance that leads to redoing, reworking, recontacting, or reviewing. Examples include missing critical data on forms and not sending out a debit card in time.
Waiting	Any time during which work is not being performed on the customer request. Examples include waiting for approval and waiting for branch feedback.
Overproduction	Producing more than required or more than a process step has the capacity to handle, resulting in the building of inventory. An example is batch processing of applications.
Unnecessary transportation	Movement of files, data, or customer requests. With every movement, there is a risk of loss or delays in processing.
Inventory	Work-in-process, representing unrecognized potential revenue. An example is applications waiting for processing.
Overprocessing	Doing more than is required from a customer's perspective.
Motion	Movement to transport information or data. An example is extra steps taken by employees to accommodate an inefficient process layout.

perfect value. For example, organizations can reengineer their processes in such a way that quality and value are embedded in them. This eliminates the need to inspect for defects at the end stage. Eliminating waste throughout the entire process leads to less human effort, space, defects, capital, and time when delivering a service. This ultimately translates into a faster response to customer needs at a lower overall cost to the organization. To attain perfect value creation, management will need to change its focus. Instead of optimizing separate technologies, assets, and vertical departments, management has to optimize the flow of products and services through the entire value stream. This will invariably require an in-depth look at the end-to-end flow that brings a product or service to the customer. Once that flow is understood, the elimination of waste and redundancies can begin. When it is deployed correctly, Lean's main deliverables are:

- A reduction in work in process (WIP), or the backlog
- Increased productivity
- Increased process capacity
- Improved area and/or organizational layouts for optimization
- Standardized operations and processes

Lean Six Sigma

Over the past century, various quality methodologies have come and gone, but some basic principles have endured. In 1913, when young Henry Ford developed his assembly-line system, he focused on standardization and taking waste out of the car manufacturing process. Over the years, the world of quality has ultimately converged on the principles that are known today as Lean and Six Sigma. Lean, with its simple approach that focuses on improving the speed and efficiency of processes, provides breadth in problem solving. On the other hand, Six Sigma is more sophisticated and offers a method for drilling deep into complex issues. Six Sigma also has a very structured approach to problem solving that is absent in Lean. By definition, Six Sigma is about enhancing the quality and accuracy of processes by reducing variation, while Lean focuses on achieving faster response times by eliminating waste. As a result, these two methodologies offer complementary tool kits; they help address the root cause of different business challenges. For example, if the goal is reducing account opening cycle time, Lean principles can help identify areas of waste to be eliminated. On the other hand, if the goal is to reduce credit card losses, Six Sigma tools provide the better fit with understanding root causes.

IMPLEMENTATION OVERVIEW

The most successful implementations of Lean Six Sigma will basically follow the path shown in Figure I.2. You can think of the implementation as a puzzle that is being put together—all the right pieces have to go in their appropriate location. The most successful rollouts have the following criteria in common. If these criteria are not met, your implementation is likely to encounter resistance and/or complications:

- The initiative uses a top-down approach.
- The organization develops an infrastructure to support the Lean Six Sigma rollout.
- Systems for obtaining customer input are established.
- There is effective training within the organization—all parties who would be affected are trained.
- Meaningful expectations are set with leaders and employees.
- Key metrics are identified.
- There is a clear link between business processes and the key metrics,

In real terms, the rollout of a Lean Six Sigma effort has three distinct phases. In the first phase, the Quality Leader aligns the effort with the company's mission, selects a focus area, and forms the organization. During the second phase, Champions are trained, metrics are developed, and projects are identified. In the third and final phase, Black and Green Belts are trained and start executing the projects.

Integral to the first phase are the milestones for building a quality infrastructure. These milestones outline at what time to engage in specific activities to ensure a successful adoption of the methodology. The first step is strategy development for the quality

Figure I.2   Lean Six Sigma Implementation

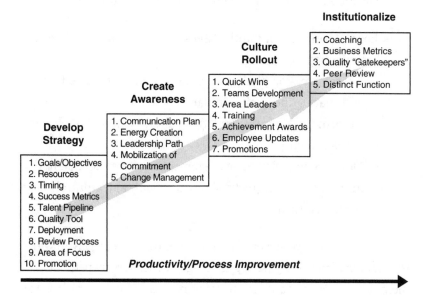

Institutionalize

Culture Rollout

1. Coaching
2. Business Metrics
3. Quality "Gatekeepers"
4. Peer Review
5. Distinct Function

Create Awareness

1. Quick Wins
2. Teams Development
3. Area Leaders
4. Training
5. Achievement Awards
6. Employee Updates
7. Promotions

Develop Strategy

1. Communication Plan
2. Energy Creation
3. Leadership Path
4. Mobilization of Commitment
5. Change Management

1. Goals/Objectives
2. Resources
3. Timing
4. Success Metrics
5. Talent Pipeline
6. Quality Tool
7. Deployment
8. Review Process
9. Area of Focus
10. Promotion

Productivity/Process Improvement

organization. Without it, the team will not have an end goal toward which it focuses all its efforts. The strategy should include the following components:

- Goals and objectives of the quality initiative
  - Resources needed
  - Timeline to be followed to ensure momentum
  - Success metrics to gauge the effectiveness of the initiative
  - A talent pipeline for training and project execution
  - Areas of focus that will both deliver quick wins and resolve chronic business issues
  - A promotion path for the Green Belts and Black Belts once they have completed their 18- to 24-month assignment

The next milestone after the strategy has been developed is to create awareness concerning the initiative. This will involve:

- Formulating a communication plan across all levels of the organization
  - Energy creation (within the organization) through education and sharing the quality initiative vision
  - Mobilizing commitment from the key stakeholders and management
  - Developing a change management road map to ensure that all points of risk (technology, political, and cultural) have been identified

This step can be the catalyst for the initiative. The way in which the organization is informed of this stage, the leadership path for staff members to work toward, and the energy creation will go a long way in creating the excitement needed for success in a critical initiative.

The third milestone is the culture "rollout." In this phase, we show the organization what it can be expect as we move further down the Lean Six Sigma path. The goal is to prove how successful and powerful the methodology can be in order to facilitate its institutionalization. The specifics that we must deliver during this phase are:

- Quick wins to maintain momentum and also overcome skepticism
  - Develop teams to get everyone involved. This helps in both identifying robust solutions and overcoming resistance.
  - Identify area leaders for continuous improvement ownership.
  - Train all levels of employees.
  - Achievement awards to ensure that hard work is recognized.
  - Promotion of Green Belts and Black Belts who have truly delivered quantifiable and meaningful benefits for the organization. This reenforces the message that the quality initiative is not going to go away, but rather that its successful leaders will be rewarded.

Of the items just listed, the one that we need to focus on most is the quick wins. It will be through these wins that the organization will feel the effectiveness and power of Lean Six Sigma. A side effect of this will be an increased demand from other departments to get involved in the initiative. Since pushing rope is ineffectual, this method of creating excitement and buy-in for the initiative is preferred. More success will come from showcasing the effectiveness of the initiative and clearly outlining how other departments can also benefit from it. This stage will also require the involvement of the company's human resources department, as many of the activities involved demand its expertise and know-how: training, promotions, developing teams, and so on. In a nutshell, the better informed coworkers are, the greater the likelihood of success with a quality initiative.

The final milestone is institutionalizing the initiative and ensuring that all projects are conducted under the rubric of Lean Six Sigma. By this point in the launch, we have sufficient staff capability to begin coaching Black and Green Belts through projects, and the business has begun implementing metrics that will guide project selection and resource allocation. The viability and worthiness of the initiative at this point is no longer in question; rather, the issue is ensuring that the organization has the tools and resources needed for continued success.

LSS ORGANIZATION STRUCTURE

For long-lasting success of the Lean Six Sigma initiative, the organization will need to have a formal structure for its deployment. This formal structure will include Green Belts, Black Belts, and Master Black Belts (see Figure I.3), as well as Champions or Sponsors. Later, in the Define phase, we will discuss the role and responsibilities of the Champion and/or Sponsor in more detail.

Figure I.3   Organization Structure for LSS Implementation

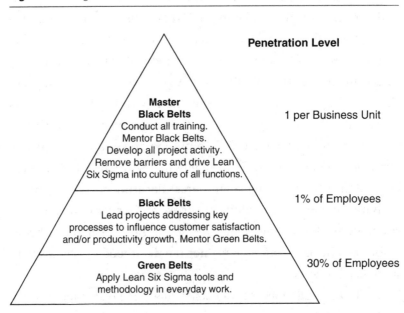

Green Belts

Green Belts are employees who have been trained in the Lean Six Sigma methodology. The expectation is that they will dedicate about 25 percent of their time to working on projects that have been identified. The role of the Green Belt is mostly one of providing invaluable expertise to Black Belts or other Green Belts. Generally Green Belts are highly regarded staff members with a good understanding of the organization in which they work. They will be provided with training, after which it is expected that they will either lead a small project or work as a team member on a larger project. Because of the fluid nature of their role, Green Belts should be able to shift easily between being a consensus builder and being a tough analyst, ensuring that work is not being postponed because of the intransigence of some uninterested party.

Over time, several of the more highly accomplished Green Belts will generally move on to become Black Belts.

Black Belts

Black Belts, unlike Green Belts, lead larger Lean Six Sigma projects. They spend 100 percent of their time working on larger-scale projects that require a full-time focus and more in-depth expertise in the methodology. They have had extensive training, have a better developed skill set, and are focused solely on the project at hand. Black Belts are a valuable resource, as they need to be competent in numerous roles. A competent Black Belt will be able to convince the toughest naysayer of the importance of working on a project. In addition to being strong analytically, she will also have the self-confidence needed to get in front of senior leaders and firmly present a business case. The best analogy is to compare a Black Belt to a polished diplomat who can sweet-talk, but also play the tough game when required.

Over time, several of your highly accomplished Black Belts will generally move on to become Master Black Belts within different units of the company.

Master Black Belt

A Master Black Belt will lead the Lean Six Sigma effort within one segment of your company. Generally, one Master Black Belt is assigned to each business unit. Master Black Belts are responsible for working with the Green and Black Belts in completing projects. The job description of a Master Black Belt is to facilitate the successful completion of all Lean Six Sigma projects in his project funnel. For this reason, a Master Black Belt must have a direct and open line of communication with senior leaders to deal with any pressing resource issues.

He must be well versed in the methodology (though it is rare that a Master Black Belt actually conducts analysis) in order to help guide the Green and Black Belts in appropriate tool usage.

Champion or Sponsor

The Champion or Sponsor leads the Lean Six Sigma effort within the entire organization. She is responsible for setting the overall quality strategy, which will require having a keen understanding of areas that are in need of improvement and/or additional resources. The Champion is often a senior-level staff member who can work easily with the Master Black Belts, Black Belts, and Green Belts in setting the overall direction for project execution. She is, in effect, a barrier buster.

PILLARS OF LONG-TERM SUCCESS

Training and successful project completion are only part of the equation for long-term success. Figure I.4 helps to outline how to ensure that the culture of continuous improvement persists way beyond the current management team. To truly achieve excellence, there has to be a standard quality culture. Lean Six Sigma, as discussed earlier, can help an organization attain that. The additional elements that are required are:

1. **Organizational commitment.** This implies buy-in from everyone, from top-level management all the way down to the salaried employee. Commitment means that everyone believes in the quality journey, understands its importance, and uses the methodology to solve everyday business issues, and that management monitors the benefits attained from the projects and activities. Commitment also means that management and executives understand their roles and

responsibilities in making the continuous improvement culture live well beyond their tenure, so they have to demand excellence and reward people when it is attained.

2. **Becoming a data-rich organization.** In order to make business decisions based on data, management and employees need access to timely and accurate process and customer data. Getting to this point can be a tedious process. While there may be copious amounts of data in an organization, the accuracy of those data may be in question, or they may not be exactly what is needed to monitor the particular issue that is being analyzed. Lean Six Sigma projects can help build the required infrastructure to get to the right data. Collection of accurate and current data requires robust business processes.

Figure I.4   The Four Pillars of a Quality Culture

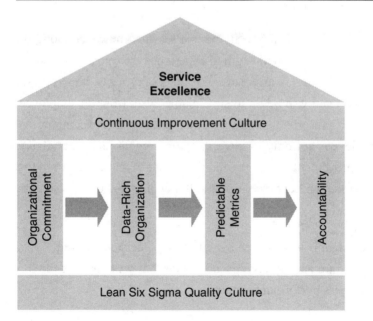

3. **Developing unbiased and predictable business metrics.**
Metrics translate the strategic goals of the business into measurable activities from the highest to the lowest level of the organization. If developed correctly, metrics allow an organization to drive a culture of accountability. The biggest challenge with developing metrics is lack of the required data.

4. **Creating a culture of accountability and acceptance.**
Accountability gives meaning and focus to the metrics of the business. However, to mitigate the risks of cultural backlash, the assistance of the human resources department should be sought. HR can help in the development and implementation of the required compensation, evaluation, training, and communication plans to achieve employee acceptance.

THE FINAL STATE

As stated earlier, Lean Six Sigma is a journey; however, along the way, an organization will begin to experience the transformation. As outlined in Figure I.5, after several rounds of projects, hopefully the leadership team will begin to shift blame away from the employees and blame poor process design. Management will have empowered the employees not only to identify improvement ideas, but also to drive improvements. In short, the final state of an organization that has embarked on Lean Six Sigma will include some of the following characteristics:

- An organization driven by data-based decision making
- Accurate and reliable process data that will support the key business performance metrics

- Line leaders and executive staff who are driven to find the root cause of problems instead of treating symptoms
- An organization that embraces and encourages a continuous improvement culture with measurable results
- An organization that is capable of making step changes instead of incremental changes

Figure I.5   Transformation from Traditional to Lean Six Sigma Thinking

Traditional Thinking		Lean Six Sigma Thinking
Management by cost	⟹	Leading by delivering value with less errors
Problem solving by gut feel	⟹	Problem solving with data
Blames people	⟹	Blames process
Company focus	⟹	Client focus
Hierarchical	⟹	Empowered teams

C   H   A   P   T   E   R

DEFINE

The Define phase (see Figure 1.1) is the starting point for all Lean Six Sigma projects. Regardless of whether the project will rely more on Lean tools and principles or on those from Six Sigma, the deliverables for this phase are the same. There are four major steps in the Define phase, each with designated tools:

Step 1: Define the project CTQ or the item or area in need of improvement.

Step 2: Outline the business case.

Step 3: Develop a high-level process map.

Step 4: Define and execute a change management strategy.

Given these steps, the main deliverables in this phase are:

- The identification of a product, process, or service that is in need of improvement

- The identification of a customer that is driving the need for improvement and defining their expectations
- A team charter with a problem statement, goal, financial benefits, scope, and required resources
- An outline of areas of risk
- The receipt of approval or sign-off from the project champion or executive sponsor

Figure 1.1   Overview of Define Steps

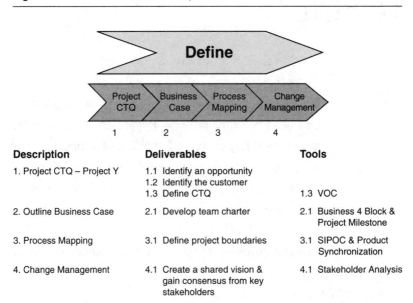

Description	Deliverables	Tools
1. Project CTQ – Project Y	1.1 Identify an opportunity 1.2 Identify the customer 1.3 Define CTQ	1.3 VOC
2. Outline Business Case	2.1 Develop team charter	2.1 Business 4 Block & Project Milestone
3. Process Mapping	3.1 Define project boundaries	3.1 SIPOC & Product Synchronization
4. Change Management	4.1 Create a shared vision & gain consensus from key stakeholders	4.1 Stakeholder Analysis

As these deliverables indicate, the Define phase can be viewed as an exploratory phase; it is during this phase that, as the project owner, you will help to determine if there is a business case that is worth pursuing. Traditionally, the Define phase is viewed as one of the more challenging phases because of the sheer amount of due diligence required to build a solid business case. If this phase is not completed accurately, the chances of success are marginal. The basic requirements are:

1. A well-defined problem statement with an accurate depiction of the frequency and magnitude of errors, issues, and defects
2. Consensus on the need for change, vision, and direction by the project champion and key stakeholders

STEP 1: DEFINE THE PROJECT CTQ OR THE ITEM OR AREA IN NEED OF IMPROVEMENT

In the first step of Define, there are three distinct deliverables:

- Defining an opportunity
- The identification of the customer
- Defining the critical-to-quality (CTQ) parameter

Defining an Opportunity

The improvement opportunity that is identified is what ultimately defines the project—what is broken, how often it breaks, and the impact on the customer and the firm. As the project owner, you will need to ensure that the opportunity has the characteristics required for a great project. What defines a great project is whether:

1. The opportunity has clear boundaries and measurable goals.
2. The opportunity is aligned with a business-critical issue or initiative.
3. The customer will feel the improvements.

A commonly asked question is, "How do I find an opportunity for improvement?" The world of opportunities is divided into two segments: internal and external. Internal improvement opportunities can be identified by:

- Brainstorming with a cross-functional team
- Analyzing core business processes, either by mapping them or by examining their historical performance (if they have been measured in the past)
- Financial analysis of the business unit
- Review of repeated business, process, product, or service issues or challenges
- Identification of business goals or metrics that have been missed or poorly executed

External opportunities are driven by your customer(s)— auditors, creditors, or consumers of your final product or service. Project ideas from external sources can be identified by:

- Conducting surveys
- Analysis of existing customer feedback
- Direct dialogue with the customers

In your discovery phase for an improvement opportunity, you may actually identify several. How can you prioritize them or eliminate some of them? Asking the following questions should help in the weeding-out process:

1. What can you do to improve the situation?
2. How important is the issue to your customer?
3. Is the opportunity or error in need of improvement measurable?

4. Are data available or easily generated?
5. Can benefits be quantified?
6. Is the process stable, or at least controllable?
7. Is the scope of the problem narrow enough to finish the improvement in four to six months?
8. Is there a sponsor or champion who is willing to provide or help you acquire the resources?

Answers to these questions should help with project selection. For example, if data are not available or easily generated, validating the problem, baselining the current state, and ultimately proving that an improvement has taken place become impossible. However, while that project should not be selected immediately, a data collection plan can be implemented in order to make the opportunity possible in the future. Also, if the scope is too large, so that the opportunity requires a substantial amount of resources (human capital as well as dollars), and/or if it may take longer than six months to complete, then perhaps it should be rescoped. But most important, whatever you choose as a project idea, it must be driven by the customer—this can be an internal or an external customer. We will discuss this idea in the upcoming section.

In the event that you are approached by a business leader with a project idea or a business issue that needs to be addressed, it is critical to note that no project idea should be accepted as factual or 100 percent accurate. What makes this phase challenging, as stated earlier, is that the burden of validating the opportunity or problem falls on the shoulders of the project leader. Validation entails both defining the problem and establishing its magnitude and the frequency of its occurrence. A well-defined problem statement helps provide a better answer to the "Who cares?" question. More on this topic will be discussed in Step 2 of the Define phase.

Identifying the Customer

Once the project opportunity has been determined, the customer(s) should be identified. Project opportunities are most often driven by managers or directors; however, while this makes the manager or director the project sponsor or champion, she is not the "customer." The customer is the recipient of the output from the process, product, or service that you will be improving during this project. Therefore, the project's customer can be internal or external. External customers are the ones who are paying the bills; they are external to the company. Internal customers are those who receive the output from business processes. As an example, if the project is to improve the quality of underwriting in the lending department, then the customers can be the operations or servicing teams (internal customers). Alternatively, if the project will focus on reducing the overall cycle time required to approve a loan, the customer is the borrower (external customer). Identifying the correct customer for the project will ensure that you have adequately captured the customer's requirements, expectations, and needs for improvement.

Defining the Critical-to-Quality Parameters

Let's start by first defining the term *critical-to-quality (CTQ)* parameter.

A CTQ is any product, process, or service *characteristic* that *satisfies* a key *customer* requirement and/or process requirement.

Because a CTQ is a process, product, or service characteristic, it has to be measurable. Examples of characteristics are speed, accuracy, timeliness, and cost. In the lending environment, customer CTQs may include time to receive a final decision and/or number of documents required to make a final decision. For opening a new account, it may be the cost of having multiple accounts at a bank or the wait time to receive a debit card. At a hospital, it may be patient wait time or accuracy of dispensing medication. The most important attributes of a CTQ are that it has to be translated directly from the *voice of the customer* (VOC) and that it must give an unbiased view of customer needs.

The challenge with most projects is that customers often tell you what they need only in vague, high-level, and nonspecific terms: "I need a quick response" or "I need more information." The challenge is to transform these customer needs into customer CTQs that are specific and measurable. Hopefully by this point it has become clear why it is important to have a well-defined customer CTQ for your project in the Define phase—because without it, you will not be able to clearly outline what process needs to be improved, and to what extent. If we were to put this discussion in terms of a mathematical equation, it would look like this:

$$Y = F(x)$$
where Y = customer CTQ or the thing we need to improve with
        Lean Six Sigma
    $F(x)$ = the internal process(es) that directly affect the
        customer CTQ

This equation can be read as Y, or the customer CTQ, is a function of x, or internal processes. To put it another way, what the customer experiences is driven by our internal processes. Once we know what the customer (internal or external) wants, we will have a better understanding of what needs to be improved in our processes, policies, products, and services.

Once we have established the customer CTQ, we will learn in upcoming phases how to link that CTQ to internal processes needing improvement.

The three milestones outlined in Figure 1.2 help to identify and define the customer CTQ:

Figure 1.2 Milestones to Determining CTQs

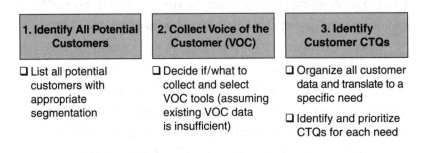

Milestone 1: Identify All Potential Customers

Customers, by definition, are the recipients of the work product at the end of a process, product, or service. The scope of the project helps define the boundaries of the process under consideration and hence the recipients of its output. Customers can be either internal (the sales team, Underwriting, Compliance, or Marketing) or external (the recipients of your services, external auditors, or the IRS). It is very common for a project to have multiple customers. One thing to consider is that you do not, and should not, treat all customers the same way, giving equal importance to their needs and expectations. Segmenting customers (based on profitability, risk, region, or complexity) is a strategy that will help you prioritize their needs and expectations. As an example, when the project is improving turnaround time in a radiology department, should patients, regulators, and doctors (all recipients of the service or end product) be treated equally when considering what to improve? When the project is changing the lending form to reduce the complexity of the process, do the voices of the regulators, lending officers, and borrowers carry the same weight? The answers may be yes, depending on the project, but that does not always have to be the case. The project goals and risks should help you prioritize what customers to focus on during the problem and solution identification stages.

Milestone 2: Collect Voice of the Customer

You may already have VOC collection processes in place, such as call centers, relationship manager client visits, or annual surveys. The data from these sources can be used to define the CTQ. However, never accept data or information as it is provided to you. The method and processes used to collect this information can affect its reliability and validity. So before analyzing the data, make sure that you understand:

- How the data were collected
- The purpose of collecting the data
- Questions asked during the data collection process
- The customers involved
- The duration of the collection process

If you don't have consistent and/or reliable data, then you may need to collect new data. There are four tools available for VOC collection:

Surveys	Focus groups
Interviews	Customer complaints

If you do have to collect VOC, make sure that you manage the customers' expectations appropriately; that is, asking for information does not always mean that you have promised to act on that information. Therefore, you must make sure that you:

- Select customers carefully.
- Explain your reason for gathering the information.
- Clarify your ability to act on the information gathered.
- Communicate your next steps to the customer.

One last note on VOC: voice of the customer information does more than identify key drivers of customer satisfaction (CTQs). VOC can also help you or the firm:

- Decide what products and services to offer or eliminate.
- Identify critical features for new or existing products and services.
- Make process management a proactive system.
- Decide where to focus your improvement efforts.
- Get a baseline measure of customer satisfaction through which to measure improvement.

Reliable, accurate, and timely collection of VOC can help business leaders make sound decisions about their products and services. It helps them understand not just what the customer wants, but how the customer utilizes the firm's existing products and services.

Milestone 3. Identify Customer CTQs

A Lean Six Sigma tool used to organize and prioritize customer CTQs is called *customer needs mapping*. This tool helps translate VOC into a customer need. There are three steps in customer needs mapping:

1. Collect voice of the customer and identify service, product, and quality issues.
2. Translate the VOC into a specific need.
3. Transform the need into a measurable process characteristic (if possible) or link it to the process that is driving dissatisfaction.

Customers are not always very good at identifying exactly what they want or need in measurable terms. The team has to conduct this translation, and the template in Table 1.1 can guide this exercise.

Table 1.1 Customer Needs Mapping Template

Voice of the Customer	Service/Quality Issue	Customer Need	Output Characteristic
What did the customer tell us?	What is wrong in the eyes of the customer based on what the customer told us and/or the data we collected?	If that is what is wrong, what does the customer need?	A concise statement of the customer need as it applies to your product, process, or service.

Here are some guidelines for completing this table:

1. **Voice of the customer.** This should be the exact statement that the customer made.
2. **Service/quality issue.** The team should agree on exactly what is the root cause of the customer's unhappiness.
3. **Customer need.**
   - Identify the need, not the solution.
   - To provide clarification, include examples.
   - If possible, use measurable terms.
   - Validate the need with the customer.
4. **Output characteristic.**
   - Be concise. A few words can adequately describe the product, process, or service output characteristic that the project will need to improve; for example, fewer customer documents or faster receipt of a debit card.
   - If possible, use measurable terms.
   - Validate the output characteristic with the project champion.

To help illustrate the use of this tool, data from the call center of a bank were collected and analyzed. The customer needs mapping tool was used to better understand the area in need of improvement, and otherwise state the customer CTQs, as shown in Table 1.2.

Table 1.2 Customer Needs Mapping for a Bank

Voice of the Customer	Service/ Quality Issue	Customer Need	Output Characteristic
"I am confused about how to sign up for online banking."	Access to online banking unclear.	Simplified online sign-up process.	• Minimize number of steps required to sign up.
"I am tired of not knowing about the status of my loan application."	Not enough communication about status of loan application.	Timely access to loan application status data.	• Provide status updates to customer at the three major milestones. • Set customer expectations—define the time required to process a loan.
"I am always being put on hold or transferred to the wrong person."	Client can't access the person he needs.	Client gets to the correct person the first time.	• Timely answer (number of seconds on hold). • Correct person the first time (yes/no).

Once the output characteristics have been defined and verified, you can select an appropriate one for your project. Usually the frequency of the problem, the impact on the customer and/or the firm, and the ease of correction are factors that are considered in prioritization.

Summary of Step 1: Define the Project CTQ

When you have completed this step, you will have identified and selected a central area for improvement. Your customer(s) and project CTQ—what is critical to satisfying your customer—has now been defined. Lean Six Sigma projects are typically focused on improving:

- Responsiveness to or communication with customers
- On-time and accurate customer deliverables
- Service performance
- Service competitiveness—price and/or value

Now that you know your customer's needs, as a project leader, you can develop the required business case, helping you gain consensus among key constituents.

STEP 2: OUTLINE THE BUSINESS CASE

The second step in the Define phase (see Figure 1.3) focuses on solidifying the business case for the project, helping to address the following questions:

- Why should the project be done?
- What are the consequences of not doing the project?
- What is expected of the team?
- How does this project fit with business initiatives and goals?

Figure 1.3   Define Phase Step 2

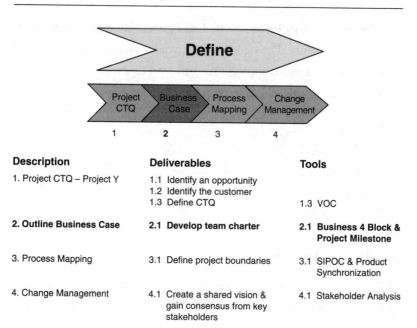

Description	Deliverables	Tools
1. Project CTQ – Project Y	1.1 Identify an opportunity 1.2 Identify the customer 1.3 Define CTQ	1.3 VOC
2. Outline Business Case	**2.1 Develop team charter**	**2.1 Business 4 Block & Project Milestone**
3. Process Mapping	3.1 Define project boundaries	3.1 SIPOC & Product Synchronization
4. Change Management	4.1 Create a shared vision & gain consensus from key stakeholders	4.1 Stakeholder Analysis

When there is no compelling case, this is usually the point at which a project idea is rejected or abandoned.

A robust business case has five components:

1. **Business case.** An explanation of why the project should be pursued.
2. **Problem and goal statements.** A description of the problem or opportunity. The project's objectives should be clear, concise, and presented in measurable terms.
3. **Project scope.** A definition of the boundaries of the process, service, or product that is in need of improvement. Included and excluded components are well outlined.
4. **Team roles.** The required resources, expectations, and responsibilities are laid out.
5. **Financial benefits.** The expected financial benefits (if any) are calculated based on expected improvements.

If these components are developed adequately, you can ensure that the project will be successful. So let's start with the problem and goal statements. The one thing to avoid is stating the problem in general and ambiguous terms; this will lead to confusion and scope creep. A good problem statement meets the SMART criteria:

S: Specific
M: Measurable
A: Attainable
R: Relevant
T: Time-bound

Problem Statement

The problem statement is an objective (quantifiable) description of the "pain" experienced by internal and/or external customers as a result of a poorly performing process or service. When writing the problem statement, consider the following questions:

- What is wrong or not meeting the customer's need or expectations?
- When and where do the problems occur?
- How big is the problem, and what is its impact?

Here is an example of a poorly written problem statement:

"Our customers are angry with us, resulting in poor customer retention."

Here is how it can be improved:

"In the second quarter (*when*), 15 percent of our customers have left the bank for another institution (*what*). The current rate of attrition is up from 8 percent to the current level of 15 percent (*magnitude*). This negatively affects our operating cash flow (*impact or consequence*).

As the project leader, when you are writing the problem statement, you need to ensure that the definition of the problem is based on observation and fact and not on assumptions. This will require the team to collect process data and analyze them to verify the problem. Assigning or prejudging a root cause in the problem statement should be avoided, as this will undermine the effectiveness of improvements. For example, do not say, "The rate of customer attrition has increased by 40 percent in the last quarter because of poor customer service."

Goal Statement

The goal statement should define the team's targeted improvement. It typically starts with a verb: reduce, increase, eliminate, or something similar. Since the root cause of the problem is not known at this point in the project, it is difficult to really know what the end result will look like. Therefore, in the Define phase, the goal statement in the business case tends to be broad; it is hard to know whether it is possible to reduce the error rate by 50 percent or to eliminate customer attrition. However, the goal statement should be refined to a more exact number after the Analyze phase, when the root cause of the problem has been identified and a strategy for improvement has been developed. Like the problem statement, the goal statement must not assign blame, assume a root cause, or prescribe a solution. At this early stage, the goal should be tied to some percentage improvement that the business or customer needs to see or feel in order to make the project worthwhile.

Project Scope

The project scope defines the boundaries of the project, that is, the start and end points of the process or service that is in need of improvement. A well-defined scope helps reduce the probability of scope creep. The three critical questions that are considered when developing the scope are:

- What process, service, or product will the team focus on?
- Is there anything that is outside the scope?
- Are there any constraints (process, IT, resources, and so on) that must be considered?

The following is an example of scope for a project focused on reducing account-opening cycle time in branches:

In Scope	Out of Scope
Retail accounts	Loans
Weekday operations	Weekend operations
"Older" branches	"New" branches
North American operations	All other geographical locations

Team Roles

A project cannot be executed solely by the Green Belt or Black Belt who is assigned to lead it. A cross-functional team, representing all the areas that will be directly affected by the project, should be formed and assigned to the project. Most often the project leader does not have the depth or breadth of knowledge of the functional area required to define the problem, collect the required data, analyze the root cause, and find the optimal solutions. In short, the project leader is not always an area expert. Having a team assigned to the Green Belt or Black Belt:

- Helps reduce the project execution timeline:
  - There will be more resources available to complete tasks.
  - The probability of rework and execution error is reduced, as tasks will be assigned to subject-matter experts.
- Ensures buy-in from the various functional areas:
  - Successful projects always lead to change, and that is not always accepted by everyone in the organization. Having a cross-functional team whose members represent the various areas that will be affected by the change ensures that these areas are involved in the problem and solution identification process. If the ideas come from the team, the probability of the improvements being accepted, implemented, and maintained is significantly higher.

Every Lean Six Sigma project has five types of roles involved in it:

- Project champion
- Project leader (Green or Black Belt)
- Key stakeholders
- Core cross-functional team
- Supplementary team

Project Champion

The champion is the individual who has initiated the improvement. Either the project idea has come from her or she sees the need for change. The champion creates the sense of urgency for the improvement. She is also known as the *barrier buster.* At every stage of project execution, the project leader may be faced with resistance—team members may be reluctant to help, area managers may not assign the required resources to the project, functional managers may reject improvement ideas, and so on. The central role of the project champion is to work within her sphere of influence to set the direction for the project and to support the Green Belt or Black Belt in its execution. She is the liaison between the project team and management, helping to create the need for change, setting the direction for the project, assigning the required resources, allocating the required funding, and removing any and all barriers to project execution. During the course of the project, she reviews progress frequently. Furthermore, once the project has ended and changes have been implemented, the project champion ensures that those changes recommended by the team are not cast aside after a few months.

Project Leader

The project leader is typically a Black Belt and is allocated to the project full-time. The Black Belt is the key planner for the project and is ultimately responsible for the deliverables: he defines the direction for project execution, determines the deliverables in each phase, creates team assignments, follows progress, and acts as a link to management. The project leader is responsible for maintaining project execution momentum—any potential risks should be escalated to the Master Black Belt or project champion. The project leader is also responsible for keeping the champion and the key stakeholders updated on the status of the project.

Key Stakeholders

Key stakeholders are individuals whose areas, processes, and teams will be directly affected by the project. They are typically part of management. It is critical to identify them during the Define phase, because without their buy-in and involvement, the probability of long-term success will be reduced. It is the responsibility of the project leader to always keep the key stakeholders abreast of the project status. Any signs of resistance from the key stakeholders should be escalated to the project champion for quick resolution.

Core Cross-Functional Team

The members of the core team are expected to allocate 10 to 15 percent of their time to supporting the project. These are functional area experts, representing the processes, services, or products that are within the scope of the project.

Supplementary Team

The members of the supplemental team act as support for the project on an as-needed basis. The time commitment from these members is minimal. Examples of supplementary team members may include HR, whose expertise will be needed during the Control phase to help ensure sustainability, Compliance to sign off on documentation or process changes, or IT to support the extraction of data from the various databases.

Financial Benefits

There will be situations in which projects that do not provide significant financial benefits will be selected for execution, for example, those dealing with compliance or regulatory issues. However, for the most part, Lean Six Sigma projects should have financial benefits associated with them. If you are focused on reducing cycle time, this should yield a reduction in touch time, and hence a reduction in labor. A reduction in cycle time also reduces inventory, such as unprocessed applications. The faster an account is opened, the faster revenue can be realized.

Calculating the expected financial benefits helps prioritize improvement opportunities and creates motivation for the team.

Business Case Example

To pull all these concepts together, Figure 1.4 shows a completed business case. A national bank's lending division is losing customers to competitors. Based on VOC data collected, the primary reason has been identified as response time. The business case has been developed by the Black Belt to be presented to the project champion and the key stakeholders.

Figure 1.4   Business Case

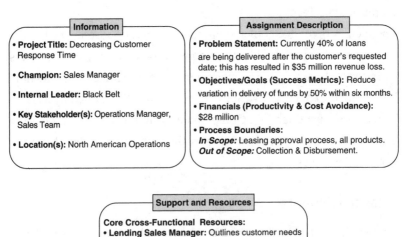

Summary of Step 2: Outline the Business Case

A well-developed business case will ensure the long-term success of the project: It communicates the project's direction to all members of the team, the champion, and the key stakeholders. The business case also helps clarify what is expected of the project team, keeps the team focused, and ensures alignment with organizational priorities.

Characteristics of a well-defined business case include:

- A clearly defined problem and goal statement
- Clearly understood defect and opportunity definitions
- No presupposed solution
- A need for improvement related to the customer's requirements
- Alignment of the project with a business strategy
- A manageable project scope—it can yield results within four to six months
- Identifiable and measurable impact
- Adequate resources assigned to the project
- A data-driven project!

STEP 3: DEVELOP A HIGH-LEVEL PROCESS MAP

To ensure that the appropriate project scope has been defined, a high-level process map of the area in need of improvement is developed (see Figure 1.5). While a very detailed process map will be constructed during the Measure phase, in the Define phase, the only key considerations are the major milestones in the process, service, or product that needs improvement.

The main benefits of a high-level process map are that it:

- Outlines the overall flow of information and material, starting with the supplier and ending with the customer.

- Provides a graphical display of the steps, events, and operations and the relationship of resources.
- Helps everyone involved in the project understand how the disparate parts of the company combine to provide a service or product.

Figure 1.5   Define Phase Step 3

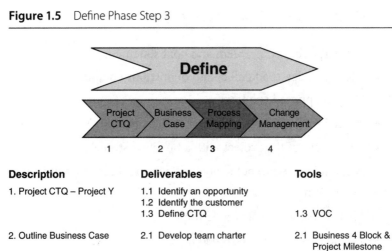

Description	Deliverables	Tools
1. Project CTQ – Project Y	1.1 Identify an opportunity 1.2 Identify the customer 1.3 Define CTQ	1.3 VOC
2. Outline Business Case	2.1 Develop team charter	2.1 Business 4 Block & Project Milestone
3. Process Mapping	**3.1 Define project boundaries**	**3.1 SIPOC & Product Synchronization**
4. Change Management	4.1 Create a shared vision & gain consensus from key stakeholders	4.1 Stakeholder Analysis

There are two tools that you can use in completing this step:

1. **SIPOC.** This is a Six Sigma tool; the acronym stands for Supplier, Input, Process, Output, Customer (see Figure 1.6).
2. **Product synchronization.** This is a Lean tool that helps define the major process milestones and the critical path.

Figure 1.6   SIPOC Overview

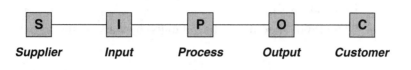

S	I	P	O	C
Supplier	*Input*	*Process*	*Output*	*Customer*

SIPOC Map

The SIPOC serves two purposes:

1. It provides a macro overview of the process or service flow and the interrelationships within a business.
2. It defines the process boundaries—the start and end points of the process in need of improvement.

How to Develop a SIPOC

Since the objective is to define a high-level view of the process in its "as-is" state, we must have the core cross-functional team involved in the development of a SIPOC.

1. As the first step, the team must agree on the start and end points of the process. The business case can help guide this discussion.
2. Working backward, list the *Customers*. Identify each customer's CTQ (accurate, timely, simple, and so on) and the *primary Output* (loans, calls, x-rays, or something else) that the customer receives from the process.
3. With the C and O of the SIPOC defined, using brainstorming techniques, the team should outline the five to seven high-level *Process* steps that result in the outputs. Process steps typically start with a verb.
4. Once the team has agreed on the process steps, the critical *Inputs* that affect the quality of the process can be identified.

5. The last step is to list all the *Suppliers* that provide inputs to the process.

6. The SIPOC should then be validated by walking the actual process.

Figure 1.7 is an example of the SIPOC for the business case outlined in Step 2 (focused on reducing loan approval cycle time).

Figure 1.7   Example of SIPOC

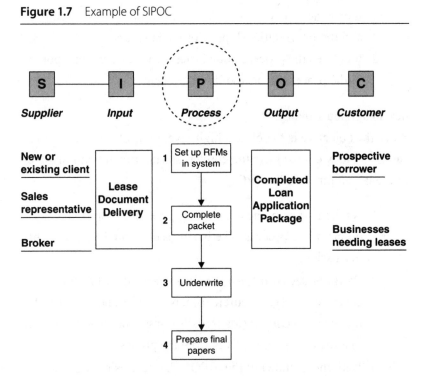

Product Synchronization Map

Product synchronization is a Lean tool that is typically used to better understand the P in the SIPOC map (see Figure 1.8). Like all Lean tools, product synchronization should be used when the project is focused on either standardizing a process or reducing its cycle time.

Product synchronization shows the *relationships* among various *process steps* (flow and applied labor) that need to come together in order to build a service or product.

Figure 1.8   Product Synchronization (Lean Tool)

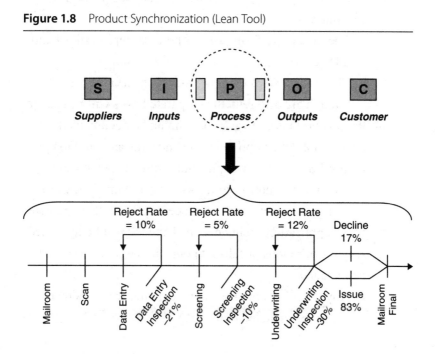

How to Develop a Product Synchronization Map

The best way to develop a product synchronization map (PSM) is by involving the core team. However, instead of brainstorming to identify the five to seven major steps, the process should be documented by "walking" the product or service through its life cycle. Here are some guidelines for developing this map:

1. Always stick to the major steps.
2. Select several examples to follow. The selected samples should be good representatives of your product or service.

3. Determine whether you need one or several PSMs. If the
   process in need of improvement produces or works on different types of products (such as securities, x-ray machines,
   or customer calls), you may need to map the processes
   separately. If:
   - The time to perform tasks or process steps is statistically
     different *or*
   - The process steps that the product or service goes
     through are different, then separate PSMs will be needed.
4. Process options and variations should be documented.
   An example of an option is data entry inspection (QA) in
   Figure 1.8. Of all new applications, only 21 percent are
   audited for data entry errors. As for variations in the process, after underwriting, the process splits, with 17 percent
   of the applications being declined and the rest being issued.
5. Any rework loops or fall-out points in the process should
   be included.
   - Any rework point or reject rate greater than 1 percent
     should be included in the map.

The product synchronization map, like the SIPOC, presents only
the high-level view of a process or service that is in need of improvement. Product synchronization provides more detail concerning the P
of SIPOC. Its main objectives are to collect information that is critical
to reducing process cycle time and increasing standardization. Using
the PSM, you can now better identify flow issues caused by:

1. Redundancies
2. Implicit or unclear requirements

3. Tricky handoffs
4. Conflicting objectives
5. Common problem areas or high rework rates

Summary of Step 3: Develop a High-Level Process Map

Once the business case has been completed, a high-level "as-is" process map of the area being focused on should be developed. This graphical representation of the process will ensure that all constituents are in agreement regarding the scope of the project and the process, product, or services involved. Clearly defining the Customer, the existing process Outputs, major Process steps, the Inputs to the process, and the individuals or entities that Supply the inputs will eliminate all assumptions and ambiguities.

STEP 4: DEFINE AND EXECUTE A CHANGE MANAGEMENT STRATEGY

The last step in the Define phase is focused on gaining consensus among key stakeholders by creating a shared need and vision for the project (see Figure 1.9). As stated earlier, the completion of the Define phase can be viewed as a "go/no-go" milestone for a project: every Lean Six Sigma project needs to receive formal approval from its champion, Master Black Belt, and finance manager (if the project has substantial financial benefits). While the team may receive formal approval, this does not always translate into success, as strong resistance from others can easily derail a sound and business-critical project. A deep understanding of the key stakeholders' position on the project will help mitigate execution risk.

Figure 1.9   Define Phase Step 4

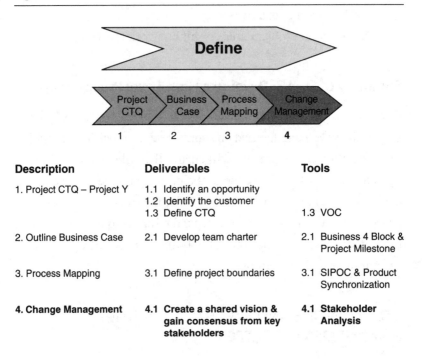

Description	Deliverables	Tools
1. Project CTQ – Project Y	1.1 Identify an opportunity 1.2 Identify the customer 1.3 Define CTQ	 1.3 VOC
2. Outline Business Case	2.1 Develop team charter	2.1 Business 4 Block & Project Milestone
3. Process Mapping	3.1 Define project boundaries	3.1 SIPOC & Product Synchronization
4. Change Management	**4.1 Create a shared vision & gain consensus from key stakeholders**	**4.1 Stakeholder Analysis**

The main benefits of a well-defined and well-executed change management strategy are that it:

- Helps an organization start and successfully complete Lean Six Sigma projects with shorter cycle time.
- Creates a shared vision of the goal and deliverables of the project.
- Ensures that you have the buy-in of key stakeholders prior to starting the project.
  - Helps identify the key stakeholders.
  - Outlines their required level of support if the project is to be a success.

- Allows for efficient implementation of solutions.
  - Increases access to required resources and data.
- Ensures that the Control portion of the project is sustainable—
  that there is an easy handoff.

Change Management Milestones and Tools

A Lean Six Sigma change management strategy has five distinct
milestones:

1. **Identifying change leadership.** Every project will need a
   champion who will sponsor the change.
2. **Developing a shared need.** The project leader and champion have to clearly articulate the need for change. It is
   best to leverage the business case. The need for change can
   be driven by a threat or opportunity, or it can be instilled
   within the organization and widely shared through data,
   demonstration, or demand.
3. **Shaping a vision.** The desired outcome of the project is
   clear, legitimate, widely understood, and shared.
4. **Mobilizing commitment.** There is a strong commitment
   from key constituents to invest in change. The team leader
   is to demand and receive management attention.
5. **Institutionalizing the change and monitoring progress.**
   Once change is started, it endures, and best practices are
   transferred throughout the organization.

There are several tools that can be used to ensure that a shared
need has been created, that all constituents have the same vision for
the project, and that all points of resistance have been identified.

Threat vs. Opportunity Matrix

The threat vs. opportunity matrix (see Figure 1.10) is a simple tool that can be utilized in creating a shared need. It can allow you to:

- Use your core team in a brainstorming session and frame the need for change as some combination of threat and opportunity over the short and long term.
- Focus on threats that may motivate some people, but only for a short period of time.

Figure 1.10   Threat vs. Opportunity Matrix

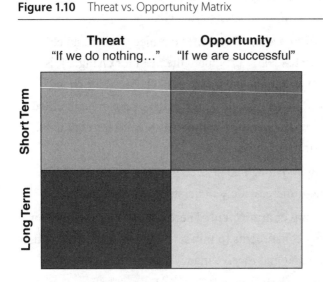

Focus on opportunities that will result in more buy-in—this is where people can see "what's in it for me."

The steps in building a threat vs. opportunity matrix are as follows:

1. The members of your team, individually or as a group, select which of the four quadrants would best create the

need for change. Each team member should share his per-
ceptions and then debate similarities and differences.

2. The team, individually or as a group, should write four to
   six statements describing the need for change.

3. If they are working individually, team members should
   read their statements, and the team should then debate and
   discuss each of them to create a statement that encompasses
   the best of all the individual efforts. This statement is then
   modified to appeal to key constituent groups (operations,
   marketing, sales, and so on).

Figure 1.11 is an example of a completed threat vs. opportunity
matrix for "reducing cycle time."

Figure 1.11   Completed Threat vs. Opportunity Matrix

	Threat	Opportunity
Short Term	• Lost clients—now • Loss of trust • Poor funds flow • Creates inefficiency • Extra concession/lost profitability • Increased application "inventory" • Higher installation cost • Pain in everyone's job	• Customer loyalty • Become number one • Comprehensive solution • Competitive advantage • Establish trust—keep it! • Retain good people • Positive impact on the future of the business
Long Term	• Loss of future sales/customers • Lost of trust/confidence • Damage to reputation • Affect the organization's business • Could affect our jobs • Lost market position	• Incremental business • Delight customers • Employee satisfaction • Better funds flow • Sales tool—positive advantage • Be creative thinkers

Elevator Speech

The elevator speech is an ideal tool for creating a vision that can be articulated in 90 seconds or less. The vision must clearly outline the future state, one for which genuine commitment can be gained from the key stakeholders. Additionally, a well-defined vision must appeal to both the "head" and the "heart" of the project's team members and key stakeholders.

The best way to create an elevator speech is by conducting a brainstorming session with the core team. The speech must provide answers to the following questions:

1. What is our project about?
2. Why is it important to do?
3. What will success look like?
4. What do we need from the key stakeholders?

Once the elevator speech has been developed, the team members should practice it to ensure that everyone conveys a similar message.

This is an example of an elevator speech for a project focused on reducing response time:

> This Lean Six Sigma project is focused on reducing our loan application response time by 85 percent. Our customers are complaining that we are not competitive and that they need a response from us within 48 hours of their completing an application. Your participation and support will be important to our success. The project manager will be setting up monthly executive updates.

Key Stakeholder Analysis

Buy-in from key stakeholders from the outset is critical to ensure project success. The key stakeholders control the resources needed for the project, have access to critical process and customer data, and will ultimately control what improvements can be implemented. Key stakeholder analysis helps define the key stakeholders and determine their current level of support and the level of support required in the future to ensure success (see Figure 1.12).

Figure 1.12   Key Stakeholder Analysis

Names	Strongly Against	Moderately Against	Neutral	Moderately Supportive	Strongly Supportive
Mike Jones		✓ ⟶		X	
Joanne Fox	✓ ⟶		X		
Tim Span				✓	
Sarah Katz			✓ ⟶ X		

Steps

1. ID key stakeholders—anyone who can block change, whose approval is required, and who has access to required resources.
2. Using ✓, outline current state of key stakeholder.
3. Using X, outline where each needs to be—gain consensus from team on both steps.
4. Outline any logical relationships between stakeholders using lines.
5. Outline gaps.
6. Once the gaps have been identified, work with the project champion and Master Black Belts to understand root cause of resistance (political, technical, cultural) and ways to overcome them.

A quick reminder: a key stakeholder is any person or group of people that is:

- Responsible for the final decision
- Likely to be affected, positively or negatively, by the outcomes you want
- In a position to assist or block your achievement of the outcomes
- An expert or special resource that could substantially affect the quality of your end product or service
- Able to have influence over other stakeholders

Summary of Step 4: Define and Execute a Change Management Strategy

Change management is not focused on the robustness of the quality strategy, whether the right candidates have been selected for Green Belt or Black Belt positions, or whether the right tools have been used to yield solutions. Rather, its central deliverable is to ensure that an environment supporting long-term success has been created—a culture of acceptance. An excellent solution without the appropriate level of buy-in will not lead to success. It is important to remember the six milestones of change management throughout project execution, starting with identifying the key stakeholders and creating a vision to mobilizing commitment by recognizing and respecting others' style.

DEFINE PHASE SUMMARY

The Define phase is one of the more challenging steps as it requires the Green Belt or Black Belt to clearly outline the need for change. Uncovering an improvement opportunity is not always a comfortable topic of discussion for all members of leadership—it inherently brings to light issues that have been overcompensated or ignored in the past. However the project leader can better facilitate discussion and remove emotion by using data in problem and goal statements. The more precise and accurate the definition of the opportunity, the better the chances that the project will be prioritized accordingly. It should also be noted that it is typically in the Define phase that a project is either accepted or rejected by the leadership team. And any rejections should not be viewed as failure by the Green Belt or Black Belt, rather it is cause for celebration. Thanks to her due diligence the company avoided investing time and money on an issue that is noncritical or blown out of proportion.

DEFINE PHASE CHECKLIST

- ☑ Define the customer (internal or external).
- ☑ Outline the customer's critical to quality (CTQ) parameter(s).
- ☑ Develop a business case—determine the problem and goal statements, milestones, scope, resources, and financial benefits.
- ☑ Define a high-level as-is state of the business process.
- ☑ Gain consensus on the business case and mobilize the required resources.

QUESTIONS TO ASK AT THE END OF THE DEFINE PHASE

1. Will my customer(s) recognize our project CTQ list?
2. Are we working on the biggest customer issue first?
3. What sources of information and data did we use?
4. What do we measure internally today to track performance?
5. Do we understand the high-level information and data flow?
6. Do we have consensus from the key stakeholders?

APPLICATION OF LEAN SIX SIGMA CASE STUDY— DEFINE PHASE DELIVERABLES

The following case study illustrates the Define phase of a Lean Six Sigma project.

Step 1: Problem Overview

The quality team at a commercial lending company is approached by the director of sales.

He is very concerned about meeting his sales numbers this year. The people on his sales team have been telling him that they are losing deals to competitors because of customer satisfaction issues: they cannot meet the customers' expectations in terms of delivering funds on time. Consequently, the customers are getting their loans from the firm's competitors.

The sales director wants to know how the company can use Lean Six Sigma to decrease its response time to the customer.

Who Is the Customer?
While the internal customer for this project is the sales director, the ultimate customer for whom the process has to improve is the individual or business requesting the loan.

What Is the Project CTQ?
Based on VOC collected by the sales director, loan applicants want a faster response from the lending company.

Step 2: Outline the Business Case

Based on data collection and interviews with key executives, the Lean Six Sigma team has developed the preliminary business case shown in Figure 1.13.

Step 3: Develop a High-Level Process Map

Using the SIPOC tool, the Lean Six Sigma team was able to better define the boundaries of the project, as shown in Figure 1.14.

Figure 1.13   Case Study Business Case

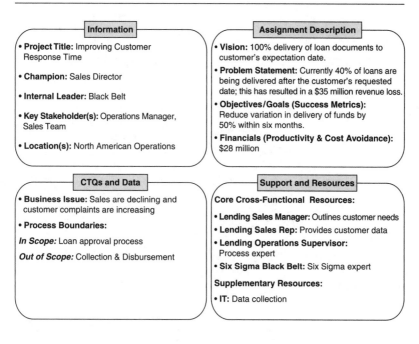

Figure 1.14   Case Study Process Map

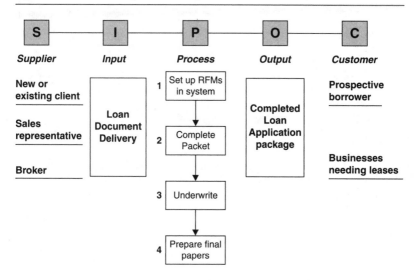

C　H　A　P　T　E　R

MEASURE

During the Measure phase (see Figure 2.1), you will develop a deep understanding of what your customer wants from you. Furthermore, you will focus on the type of data needed and ensure that you have the correct mechanism for gathering these data if you do not already have them in your possession. The main steps in the Measure phase are:

Step 5: Define the CTQ characteristics (project Y)
Step 6: Outline performance standards
Step 7: Develop a data collection plan
Step 8: Validate the measurement system

Much like the Define phase, the Measure phase has distinct deliverables associated with these four steps:

- Drill down on customer critical-to-quality parameters (CTQs), also known as the big Y to little y, where little y is the process(es) that has the largest impact on the big Y (customer CTQ).

Figure 2.1   Overview of Analysis Steps

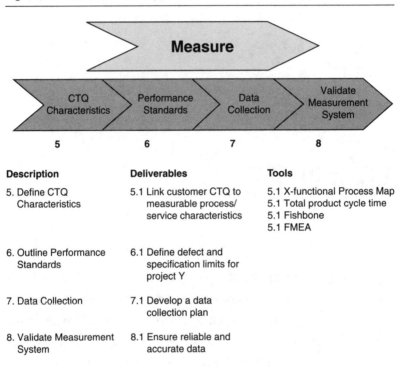

Description

5. Define CTQ
   Characteristics

6. Outline Performance
   Standards

7. Data Collection

8. Validate Measurement
   System

Deliverables

5.1 Link customer CTQ to
    measurable process/
    service characteristics

6.1 Define defect and
    specification limits for
    project Y

7.1 Develop a data
    collection plan

8.1 Ensure reliable and
    accurate data

Tools

5.1 X-functional Process Map
5.1 Total product cycle time
5.1 Fishbone
5.1 FMEA

- Performance standard for big Y.
- A detailed process map
- A definition of the defect, developed by reviewing the competition and customer requirements
- Validate that the defect definition can be measured (data source validated)
- Establish and distinguish between data types involved (discrete/attribute vs. continuous/variable)
- Initiation of the data-gathering process
- Validation of the accuracy and reliability of the data collected

Looking at these deliverables, the Measure phase is better defined as one that allows you to develop a better understanding of the project.

STEP 5: DEFINE THE CTQ CHARACTERISTICS (PROJECT Y)

As you progress through this phase, you will link the customer requirement (the project CTQ) to the element(s) of the process that need to be improved because they have the largest impact on the CTQ (the project Y). For example, you may know that your project CTQ (or what the customer has asked of you) is "on-time delivery of funds"; by the end of this step, through the use of various tools, you will have determined that the largest driver of "on-time delivery" is the "loan approval process." And that is your project y—the cycle time required to approve applications for loans. Asking a series of questions will guide you on the journey of moving from the project big Y (what the customer wants) to the little y (the process with highest impact on the customer want):

What am I trying to improve?
What does the customer deem essential?
How do I set up a project to meet the customer's needs?

The first question may seem obvious and easy to answer, but in reality, answering it may be a more complex exercise. Deciding exactly what it is you are trying to improve will force you to understand what your customer deems critical and what processes or process elements affect the customer's expectation. To help you arrive at the answer to these questions, specific tools are available:

• Process map

- Fishbone diagram
- FMEA

X-Functional Process Map

Process mapping is a powerful tool in developing an understanding of how a business is performing and, more important, how it is not. Through the use of the two different forms of process maps we outline here, you can get a "street-level" view of your operations. The central benefits of process mapping are that it:

1. Provides the ability to uncover problem areas in your business, particularly if they have historically been overlooked.
2. Enables the entire group to have a clear view of how a particular operation is failing to meet customer needs.
3. Helps pinpoint the data that you need—and may not possess.
4. Eliminates the perception of how a process works by documenting how it actually flows.

It is essential that you depict things (operations, process flow, and so on) as you see them while you are conducting your research. You must not attempt to gloss over anything. Rather, you must show things as they actually occur in your organization.

The rule of thumb for process mapping is that you need to become the thing that you are trying to map—the loan application, the CT machine you manufacture, or the new employee you are trying to hire. Every transformation, waiting point, inspection, rework, reentry, and anything else you find must be documented. The devil is always in the details. The toughest part of process mapping is *not* putting one process step in front of the other, but determining the level of detail in which to document the process. For that, the only guidance that can be provided is that the level of process detail should be defined by what it is that you are trying to fix. If, when you have documented the process, the problem areas are not clear, that may be a good indication that the documentation was not detailed enough. However, it could also mean that you have not selected the right process.

How to Start with Process Mapping

Before you can get into the details of the process, you first need to understand the flow from the start to the end. The following steps will help:

1. **Determine the scope.** This means that you have to have a firm understanding of the boundaries of the business issue you are tackling. This step is critical if you are to have a successful undertaking. The SIPOC map created in the Define phase should help. Clarifying for the team (and yourself) the beginning point of the process you are mapping and at exactly what stage you will stop prevents scope creep and keeps the exercise at a realistic level.

2. **Determine the steps.** Develop an understanding of what happens in the area you have targeted. You can use your team to develop this map (assuming that your team consists of people who actually do the work). Get your team members to talk about the process. Don't worry about the order or the priorities. Just list the steps and use verbs to describe the activities.

3. **Identify and list your key inputs and outputs.** Whenever possible, for each step you define, outline the key inputs and outputs and who provides them.

4. **Arrange the steps in order.** This is a rather simple task, but you cannot make mistakes when you represent what happens, as doing so may inhibit your ability to make changes.

5. **Assign symbols to your mapped steps.** Figure 2.2 shows the various symbols that are commonly used.

- Rectangles for steps
- Ovals for start and stop
- Diamonds for decisions

Figure 2.2   Process Map Symbols

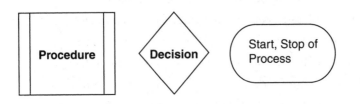

Once you have completed the process map, you need to validate what you have captured and add the required details. In many cases, the initial picture that is captured does not reflect what actually happens—remember that people just listed the steps from memory. Therefore you must:

- Walk the process. This will ensure that you have not missed any critical but often overlooked steps.

- Start adding the process steps and details that the team members forgot to mention or assumed were common knowledge.
- Ensure that every arrow has a beginning and an end point.
- Ensure that all decision points have an ending.
- Ask the following questions:
  - What happens if ...?
  - What could go wrong?
  - Who ...?
  - How ...?
  - When ...?

Once you have completed these steps, you should update the map. Figure 2.3 shows an example of an automated customer account transfer (ACAT) process at a brokerage firm.

Figure 2.3 ACAT Process Map

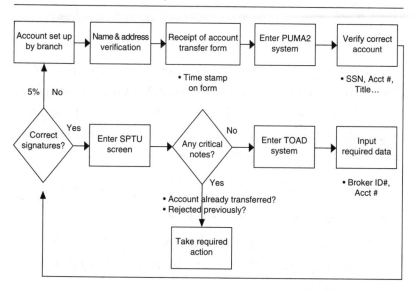

Process Mapping Summary

If process mapping is done correctly—if all the steps were identified and the documentation was based on actual observation—the process map will serve as the foundation of your problem solving. A good process map will help you:

- Identify all non-value-adding steps—activities that add cost or time but no value.
- Drill down from the customer CTQ to the project y—the area in the process that makes the largest contribution to the problem.
- Uncover steps that are "hidden" or highly customized.
- Outline areas where data collection is needed.
- Outline the *existence* or *lack* of required controls.
- Identify all the "re's" in the process:
  - Rework
  - Revise
  - Repeat
  - Review

Fishbone Diagram

A fishbone diagram, also known as a cause-and-effect diagram, is a commonly used tool to identify critical Xs. Process parameters that have the highest impact on process performance. It is used as a visual display to enable the team to understand the contributors to a particular problem. The fishbone is used to:

- Ensure that all possible causes are being considered.
- Tap into process experts' knowledge.
- Ensure that the true problem has been identified.
- Identify and gauge the impact and the ease of implementation for each identified cause.

Figure 2.4 shows a fishbone template and an impact vs. implementation scoring guideline. In this case, six major categories of causes have been identified: policies, procedure, people, environment, IT systems, and measurement. While you can use this as a template, the major categories can change to better fit the needs of your project.

Figure 2.4   Fishbone Diagram

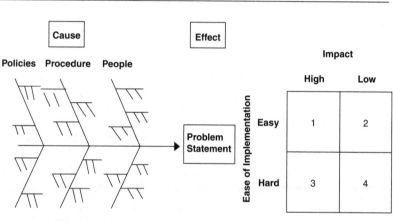

How to Generate a Fishbone

The fishbone is one of the easiest and most user-friendly Six Sigma tools—all it requires is brainstorming with a cross-functional team of people representing the entire process. Keeping the team focused on the problem statement and the list of elements that may be potential drivers of the problem is all that is needed. A sparse diagram or empty branches may indicate that the problem is not well understood or that the appropriate team may not have been assembled. Remember that a category with many causes may be a good place to focus your data collection, and that some suggested categories may end up not having any entries. After all the potential causes have been identified by the team, those causes should be ranked 1-4 based on the Impact vs. Ease of Implementation grid. Figure 2.5 is an example from a hospital that is focused on improving the throughput in the radiology department. Once the key drivers of throughput are agreed on, the team can proceed with its investigation and data collection.

Figure 2.5   Fishbone Diagram for Radiology Department

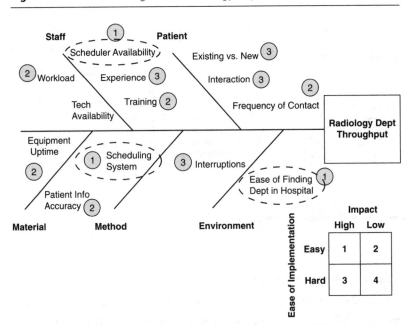

Failure Modes and Effects Analysis

A simple, versatile, and powerful tool, failure modes and effects analysis (FMEA) allows a team to identify defect(s) in the process that should be eliminated and/or reduced (Figure 2.6). The goal of FMEA is to outline process steps that are at risk of contributing to failure.

FMEA is a structured approach to:

- Identifying the ways in which a process can fail to meet critical customer requirements
- Estimating the risk of specific causes for these failures
- Evaluating the current control plan for preventing these failures from occurring
- Prioritizing the actions that should be taken to improve the process

Figure 2.6 Building an FMEA

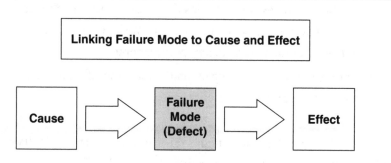

Main Purpose and Benefits of FMEA

While the focus of the team in the Analyze phase is on identifying critical elements that are driving customer dissatisfaction, additional benefits derived from FMEA include the ability to:

- Document and track actions that are taken to reduce risk.
- Identify value-adding and non-value-adding steps.
- Identify process variation caused by training or personnel—high customization.

- Improve the quality and reliability of products or services.
- Reduce product development time and cost.

How to Build an FMEA

As a tool that requires the input and expertise of a cross-functional team in its development, FMEA is led by the person(s) responsible for the system, product, or service that is need of improvement. For each process step, the team is looking to identify the:

1. **Failure modes.** The ways in which a request or process can fail to meet specs.
2. **Potential causes.** Deficiencies that could result in a failure mode. Potential causes are sources of variability and are normally associated with key process inputs.
3. **Potential effect.** The impact on the customer if a failure mode is not prevented or corrected.

Once the team has identified a failure mode, a risk priority number (RPN) is calculated for each failure mode. The equation for RPN is as follows:

$$RPN = Severity \times Occurrence \times Detection$$

The maximum value for RPN is 1,000, as each element (severity, occurrence, and detection) is ranked on a scale from 1 to 10, as shown in Table 2.1.

In summary, the three main milestones and the corresponding activities within each milestone required to create an FMEA are outlined in Figure 2.7.

Table 2.1   RPN Calculation

		Scoring	
RPN Calculation	**Definition**	**1 (min)**	**10 (max)**
Severity	How significant is the impact of the *effect* on the customer?	Least significant	Most significant
Occurrence	Likelihood of cause of the failure mode to occur?	Not likely to occur	Likely to occur
Detection	Likelihood that the current system can detect the cause or failure mode if it occurs?	Likely to detect	Not likely to detect

Figure 2.7   FMEA Milestones

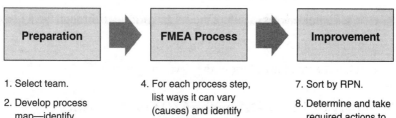

Preparation	FMEA Process	Improvement
1. Select team.	4. For each process step, list ways it can vary (causes) and identify associated failure modes and effects.	7. Sort by RPN.
2. Develop process map—identify process steps.		8. Determine and take required actions to reduce RPNs.
3. List key process inputs and outputs to satisfy internal and external customer requirements.	5. Assign severity, occurrence, and detection rating to each cause.	
	6. Calculate risk priority number (RPN) for each potential failure mode scenario.	

Example

In the brokerage sector, it is very critical to purchase securities or mutual funds on the day that the customer has requested that they be purchased. However, as in other processes, there are times when requests are not carried out on a timely basis. A team of Green Belts documented the process for opening a fee-based account from the branch all the way to the back office where securities are purchased. Table 2.2 outlines a small section of the FMEA.

FMEA Summary

FMEA is a tool for assessing process risk based on the expertise and knowledge of a cross-functional team.

- FMEA can be used anytime on any product, process, or service when:
    - Risk assessment is needed.
    - There is a need to better understand the root causes of failure.
    - There is a need to identify failure points.
- It helps link causes to failure modes and prioritize through the RPN.
    - The higher the RPN, the higher the risk.
- It can be used throughout the DMAIC process.

Summary of Step 5: Define the CTQ Characteristics (Project Y)

The tools discussed in this step, process mapping, the fishbone diagram, and FMEA, can be used to narrow down the scope of the project. While the problem statement outlined in the Define phase can encompass an entire process, service, or product, Step 5 is intended to help the team better define a focal point. As outlined in the fishbone example, while the project is focused on increasing throughput in the radiology department, the team's consensus was that the scheduling system was the largest contributor to the problem.

Table 2.2 Example RPN Calculation

						Prepared by: Tom M			Page ___ of ___

Process or Product Name: Fee-Based Account Opening

Responsible:

Prepared by: Tom M

FMEA Date (Orig) _____ (Rev) _____

Process Step	Potential Failure Mode	Potential Failure Effects	Severity	Potential Causes	Occurrence	Current Controls	Detection	RPN	Actions Recommended
Enter Account no.	Wrong Account no.	Change someone else's account	9	Incorrect info on application	3	No current controls	10	270	
	Invalid Account no.	Cannot proceed with new account opening process	9	Incorrect info on application	4	No current controls	4	144	
Check Funding	Balance = 0	Funds cannot be purchased	8	Customer did not transfer required funds	3	System notification	1	24	
	Balance > 0 but has securities	Account cannot be opened	3	Customer has not liquidated account	6	System notification via reporting	2	36	
Enter Value	Entered value > existing	Incorrect amount of securities are purchased	9	Appropriate funds were not transferred	4	Fund purchasing department verification process	4	144	
		Appropriate amount of securities are not purchased	9	One account used to fund multiple & sum exceeds actual	6	None	9	486	

83

STEP 6: OUTLINE PERFORMANCE STANDARD

A performance standard translates a customer need into a clear and measurable characteristic (see Figure 2.8). Once we know what is acceptable, we can then define a defect. Elements of a good performance standard include:

Figure 2.8   Overview of Analysis Steps

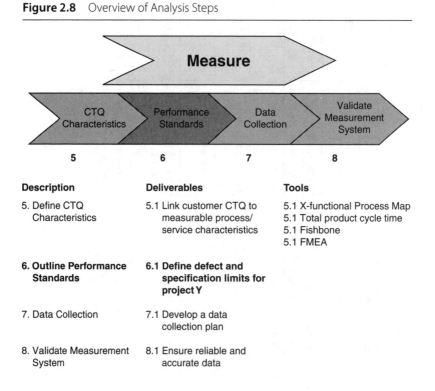

Description	Deliverables	Tools
5. Define CTQ Characteristics	5.1 Link customer CTQ to measurable process/ service characteristics	5.1 X-functional Process Map 5.1 Total product cycle time 5.1 Fishbone 5.1 FMEA
6. Outline Performance Standards	**6.1 Define defect and specification limits for project Y**	
7. Data Collection	7.1 Develop a data collection plan	
8. Validate Measurement System	8.1 Ensure reliable and accurate data	

- **Operational definition.** This is a precise description that removes ambiguity concerning a process. It provides a clear way to measure that process. An operational definition is key in getting a value for the CTQ that is being measured.

- **Target.** This is where a process or product is aimed. If there were no variation in the process, this is the value that would always be achieved.
- **Specification limits.** This is the amount of variation in the process, product, or service that a customer is willing to tolerate. It is usually shown by upper and lower bands (specification limits) that, if surpassed, will cause rejection or dissatisfaction by the customer.
- **Defect definition.** A defect is anything that results in customer dissatisfaction or nonconformance.

Example

At this point in the project, we know that the customer wants the funding faster. In order to attain this goal, we must reduce the time it takes to enter customer application data in the loan application process. What we need to determine is:

- How does the customer measure or define cycle time?
- By how much does the time need to be reduced?
- How will we measure cycle time?
- How much variation will the customer accept?

Operational Definition

There are two questions that need to be answered with regard to the operational definition:

1. What are the start and end of the process from the customer's perspective?
2. How should we measure the process?

There has to be consensus and complete alignment on how the process performance should be measured.

Here is an example of complete misalignment, better known as having only an internal view of your process performance.

Definition of cycle time for loan application:

Customer's definition: The start of the application process is defined as the minute a customer contacts a sales rep, and the process ends when a final decision is received from the company.

Company's definition: The start of the application process is defined as the time when all the required documentation has been collected from the customer, and the process ends when a final decision is mailed out to the customer.

Good operational definitions are always developed from a customer's perspective (see Figure 2.9).

Figure 2.9   Develop Operational Definition from the Customer's Perspective

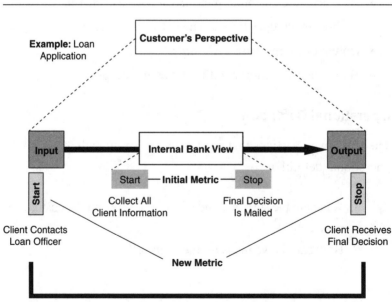

Measure the Process

When you are thinking about data collection, there are two types of data to consider, discrete and continuous, and the type that you are dealing with will matter.

Some of the characteristics of discrete data are:

- With these data, you count the frequency of occurrence, such as the number of times something happens or fails to happen, yes or no, or a count of defects.
- The measurement is not capable of being meaningfully subdivided into more precise increments.
- The sample size required to characterize a discrete product or process feature is much larger than that required when continuous data are used.

The primary characteristic of continuous data is:

- The measurement scale can be meaningfully subdivided into finer and finer increments with greater and greater precision.

It is important that you collect continuous data whenever possible. Why is the data type important? Continuous data can help outline the *magnitude* of the problem—that is, the level of variation. In an account opening process cycle time analysis, for example, continuous data allow you to know how many accounts were opened late and *how* late. Discrete data also limit the choices of potential data displays and analysis tools. Table 2.3 gives some examples of discrete vs. continuous data for a CTQ.

Table 2.3 Data Types

CTQ Type	Continuous	Discrete
Dimensions	Actual dimensions	In/out, pass/fail
Time	Actual time	Over/under estimate
Money	Actual amount	Over/under budget
Quality	Pounds of scrap	Number of scrapped parts

Specification Limits

How much variation will a customer tolerate? The answer will determine your specification limits. In the loan application project, based on customer feedback, it was determined that customers expect a final decision from the company within three days of talking with the loan office representative. Therefore, by definition, the upper specification limit is three days—any answer provided to the customer beyond three days can lead to dissatisfaction. And since providing a customer with an answer in less than than three days will not cause any complaints, there is no lower specification limit. However, in other industries, like manufacturing and pharmaceuticals, there will be both upper and lower specification limits. When mixing compounds to produce a specific drug, the manufacturer needs to ensure that it doesn't put in too little or too much of a particular ingredient. Hence, there are upper and lower specification limits.

Target Performance

Where should the process be centered? If there were no variation, what is the value that we would want the process to perform at? In the case of the loan application, we know that we cannot exceed three days, and we also know that there is always variation in the process (variation in the volume of incoming applications, the complexity of the various loans, the number of employees who are on holiday, and so on), so if we targeted our process at three days, we would be sure to create dissatisfaction in some customers. The process target is a value somewhere in between the lower and upper specification limits. At this stage, we can determine a number based on historical performance and customer expectation. A more robust value will be calculated in the Improve and Control phases once we determine the process capability (variation in relation to the customer need). In the case of the loan approval process, the operations manager was confident that the firm could center the process around 36 hours; that is, with a high level of confidence, the firm can provide a response to the customer 36 hours after contact with the loan officer.

Defect Definition

By definition, a defect is anything that results in either customer dissatisfaction or nonconformance.

Now, putting the whole picture together for the loan approval process, the operational definition for the project is:

> The *target* time for completing the documentation of a commercial loan is 36 hours. Anything completed beyond 72 hours will be deemed a *defect* (see Figure 2.10).

Figure 2.10 Performance Standard

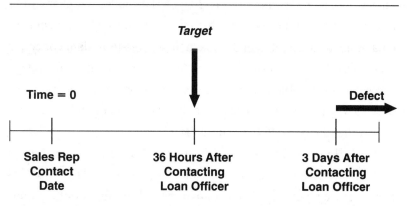

Summary of Step 6: Outline Performance Standard

The goal of a performance standard is to translate the customer need into a measurable characteristic. If done correctly, the performance standard helps in translating the voice of the customer to the voice of the process: it helps to provide answers to questions like: What does the customer want? What is a defect? What is a good process or product?

Key elements that have to be defined in order to develop a good performance standard are:

- Operational definition
- Target
- Specification limits
- Defect definition

STEP 7: DEVELOP A DATA COLLECTION PLAN

With the process that is in need of improvement defined, the team now has to determine the data that are required to analyze the performance of that process (see Figure 2.11). A data collection plan will be required regardless of whether the team is able to rely on historical data or needs to develop and implement a short-term data collection process. A data collection plan provides a clear, documented strategy for gathering reliable data for the project and gives all the members of the team a common reference point for the collection.

What data should the team collect?

While the team may still be focused on the process output or what the customer needs or wants (the project CTQs), such as faster service, getting the right answer the first time on the phone, or no defects in the product, this is also the ideal time to start collecting data on process variables and process input variables (Xs) (see Figure 2.12).

Data collection can be costly and time-consuming, and so it is best to collect what the team may deem critical now, as this will help you save time in the Analyze phase. The best way to generate a good list of possible Xs is by using tools like process mapping, brainstorming, and a fishbone diagram. These tools help you identify points or variables that may contribute to the variation or customer issue that you are trying to resolve.

Figure 2.11 Overview of Analysis Steps

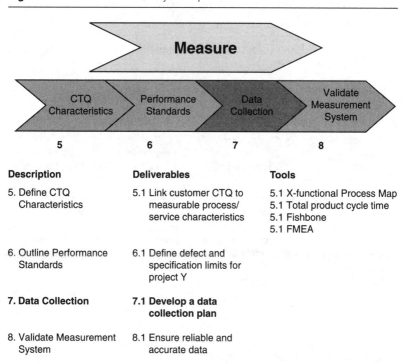

Description	Deliverables	Tools
5. Define CTQ Characteristics	5.1 Link customer CTQ to measurable process/ service characteristics	5.1 X-functional Process Map 5.1 Total product cycle time 5.1 Fishbone 5.1 FMEA
6. Outline Performance Standards	6.1 Define defect and specification limits for project Y	
7. Data Collection	**7.1 Develop a data collection plan**	
8. Validate Measurement System	8.1 Ensure reliable and accurate data	

Figure 2.12 Data Collection for Process Xs and Ys

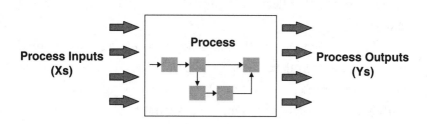

Data Collection Plan

When developing a data collection plan, there are four key milestones to consider (see Figure 2.13):

1. Establishing data collection goals
2. Developing operational definitions and procedures
3. Ensuring data consistency and stability
4. Actual data collection and monitoring

Figure 2.13   Data Collection Milestones

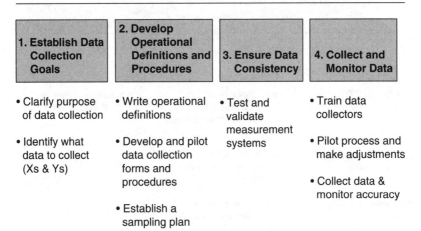

The main objectives of the first step are to ensure that you have a complete list of the process Ys and Xs that you want to collect. This step is also focused on making certain that there is consensus on why the team needs to collect the data—what are we trying to measure and gauge?

For the second step, the team needs to define an *operational definition* for each data element—a precise description of how to get a value for the characteristic that you are trying to measure so that there is no ambiguity concerning what to measure and how to measure it. In this step, it is also important to develop a data collection template or form. The last element to be considered in this step is *data sampling.* It is often impossible, impractical, or too costly to collect *all* the data from every aspect of your process. When there are too many data (thousands of items to evaluate), when too much time would be required to investigate all the data (each event lasts weeks or months), or when measurement is costly (it involves a destructive process or single-use items), it is important to consider data sampling.

A good sampling plan must be:

- Representative of all segments (for example, locations, sizes, days of the week, months, or shifts)
- Of adequate size—while there are mathematical equations that can determine the exact sample size needed, the guidelines in Table 2.4 can provide a rough estimate
- Free from bias. Avoid collecting only when doing so is convenient, omitting shifts or collecting for a short time (ignoring long-term effects) or from responsive employees

Table 2.4 Adequate Sample Sizes

Statistic	Minimum Sample Size
• Average	30
• Standard deviation	30
• Proportion defective (P)	300
• Histogram or Pareto chart	50–100
• Scatter diagram	50–100
• Control chart	25–35

The last point to consider in data sampling is the scheme that you will use to sample. There are four possible options:

- **Random.** With this option, each unit has an equal chance of being selected. It is a good option for homogeneous populations (see Figure 2.14).
- **Stratified random.** When data are needed from multiple areas, this ensures that all groups that are of interest are adequately represented. The sample size for each group is generally proportional to the relative size of the group (see Figure 2.15).

Figure 2.14   Random Sampling

Population   **Sample**

XXX**X**XXXXXX
XXXXX**X**XXXX
XXX**X**XXXX**XX**   **XXXXX**
XXXXXX**X**XX...

Figure 2.15   Stratified Random Sampling

| | **Population** | | **Sample** |
Group	**Units**		
Compliance	XX**X**XX		**X**
Back Office	XX**X** XX**X** XXX **X**XX		**XXX**
Legal	X**X**X XXX X**X**		**XX**

- **Rational subgrouping.** Rational subgroups are samples from similar processes (for example, comparing cycle time from production lines 1, 2, and 3) or items from the same process over time (for example, morning shift vs. afternoon shift). The word *rational* implies there is reasoning behind the choice of subgroup size and interval. If selected correctly, subgroups help identify variation within the group and between the subgroups (see Figure 2.16).

Figure 2.16 Rational Subgroup Sampling

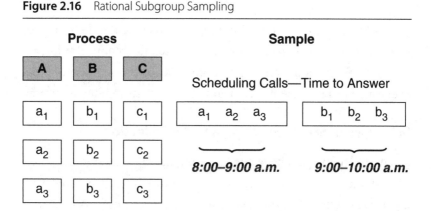

- **Systematic sampling.** Sample every nth unit (for example, every fourth unit). This method helps guard against time-related biases (see Figure 2.17).

Milestone 3 of the data collection plan ensures that the way in which the data have been collected is reliable and accurate. This concept will be covered in more detail in the upcoming chapter.

As for the last step in the data collection plan, once the team has ensured that the measurement system is adequate for the data

Figure 2.17   Systematic Sampling

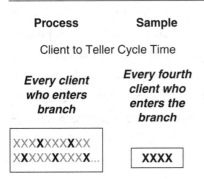

that needs to be collected, the people collecting the data need to be trained on how, when, and where to track the required information. It is best to conduct a pilot of the data collection to ensure that everyone has been adequately trained prior to full implementation.

Summary of Step 7: Develop a Data Collection Plan

A data collection plan helps the team provide the answer to questions like: What data do we need? What is the time frame for collecting them? Who will collect the data? Using what mechanism? A good data collection plan provides a clear, documented strategy for gathering reliable data for the project. While developing the plan, the team needs to ensure that the collection process yields reliable and accurate data. It also needs to ensure that the data are representative of the entire population, that the sample is of adequate size, and that the data are free of biases. The quality of the data is critical, as they are used in the Analyze phase to enable the team to better understand the capability of the process and help uncover opportunities for improvement. Poorly collected data can steer the team in the wrong direction, with adverse impact on the company.

STEP 8: VALIDATE THE MEASUREMENT SYSTEM

Data are only as good as the measurement system that measures them (see Figure 2.18). Data collection is a process, and as with any process, there will be variations in it. It is important that the measurement process is accurate and that the variation in the measurement process is minimized and consistent over time. The ability of a data collector to get the same response time after time and the degree of accuracy of a measurement process must be determined and quantified for both discrete and continuous data collection plans (see Figure 2.19). The question under consideration is, "Is the variation (spread) within my

Figure 2.18   Overview of Analysis Steps

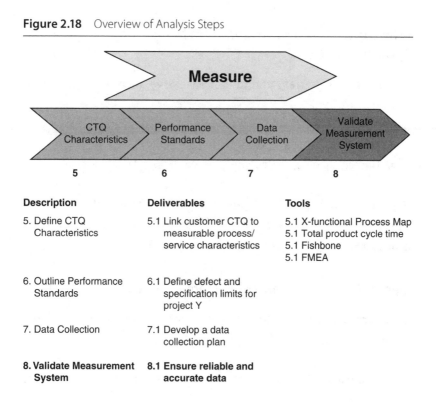

Description	Deliverables	Tools
5. Define CTQ Characteristics	5.1 Link customer CTQ to measurable process/ service characteristics	5.1 X-functional Process Map 5.1 Total product cycle time 5.1 Fishbone 5.1 FMEA
6. Outline Performance Standards	6.1 Define defect and specification limits for project Y	
7. Data Collection	7.1 Develop a data collection plan	
8. Validate Measurement System	**8.1 Ensure reliable and accurate data**	

measurement system too large to allow me to study the current level of process variation?" *The goal is to minimize the measurement variation so that the actual process variation can be observed.*

Figure 2.19   Variability

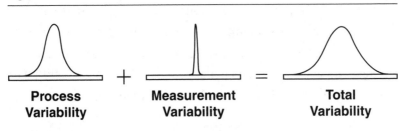

| **Process Variability** | **Measurement Variability** | **Total Variability** |

Why Do We Need to Understand Measurement System Variation?

If measurement system variation is excessive, there is an *increased* risk of:

- Good service being rejected (a cost issue)
- Bad service being accepted (a quality issue)

It is important that we know how much of the *measured variation* of a process is due to the *variation in the actual process* and how much is due to *variation in the measurement system.*

Elements of Measurement System Analysis

There are two types of measurement system errors: those involving accuracy and those involving precision.

- **Accuracy.** Do the measurements match the actual value or *expert data*?

- **Precision.** This type of error has two subcategories:
  - **Repeatability.** Do we get the same results repeatedly when the same person makes the same measurement on the same unit with the same measuring equipment?
  - **Reproducibility.** Do we get the same results when two or more people measure the same characteristic on the same unit with the same measuring equipment?

To find the answers to these questions, we must first determine whether the measurement system tests will be conducted on discrete or continuous data. The analysis will depend on the data type.

The following is an example of attribute measurement system analysis.

Compliance with Form Codes

The operations team at a brokerage firm completes the account opening process once all the documents have been received from the branches. There have been complaints from the branches that accounts are not being opened on time, but the operations team is voicing concern that the incoming documents are incomplete (leading to rework). The Lean Six Sigma team needs to improve this process. However, before it can investigate the root cause of the issue, it first has to ensure that the measurement system is adequate. In this case, the operations employees who receive the documents count the number of errors. The measurement system analysis will help ensure that the error rate that the operations team is calculating is a true reflection of the number of mistakes being made by the branches.

Calculating Accuracy

Accuracy is the difference between the *observed* measurement and a *master*, *standard*, or *expected value*. For discrete data, it is calculated by counting the number of instances in which the "wrong" answer was observed.

The Lean Six Sigma team created a set of the documents that the operations team would typically receive from the branches. It deliberately made specific errors and omissions on the documents in order to help create a "master standard" for the measurement system analysis. The Lean Six Sigma team then asked a member of the operations team to review the master standard documents and count the number of errors. Table 2.5 shows the comparison.

In this case, for two documents, new account and home equity loan application, the error count was incorrect.

$$\text{Accuracy} = 2 \text{ miscounts}/10 \text{ forms} = 80\%$$

Table 2.5   Accuracy

Form Name	Master Standard Count of Errors	Data Collector's Count of Errors
New Account	11	10
Wire Transfer	13	13
Brokerage	12	12
Car Application	10	10
Home Equity Loan Application	15	11
Compliance	1	1
Legal	1	1
ACAT Form	5	5
IRA Application	99	99
Business Account	0	0

Calculating Precision: Repeatability

Repeatability is the variation that occurs when *one person* repeatedly measures the *same unit* with the *same* measuring *device*. For discrete data, this is calculated by counting the number of times the same result is achieved for a given unit (percent agreement) for each person.

The Lean Six Sigma team asked two operations team members to review the documents twice, in a difference sequence. The number of errors and omissions for each document was to be recorded each time. The question is, "Can the operations person match his or her results each time?" It is important to note that repeatability reflects consistency, not correctness. Thus, an operations person may have counted the number of errors on a document incorrectly, but as long as he or she counts them incorrectly every time, while we have an accuracy issue, we don't have a repeatability issue. Table 2.6 shows the results.

Table 2.6   Repeatability

		Data Collector 1		Data Collector 2	
Form Name	**Master Standard**	**Adam 1**	**Adam 2**	**Sarah 1**	**Sarah 2**
New Account	11	11	10	11	11
Wire Transfer	13	13	13	13	13
Brokerage	12	12	12	12	12
Car Loan Application	10	10	10	10	9
Home Equity Loan Application	15	15	15	15	15
Compliance	1	1	1	1	2
Legal	1	1	1	1	1
ACAT Form	5	5	5	5	3
IRA Application	99	99	99	99	99
Business Account	0	0	0	0	0

While there is only one instance in which Adam's results don't match, there are three in which Sarah's don't.

$$\text{Repeatability} = \text{agreement within operator/total units}$$
$$\text{Adam's overall repeatability} = 9/10 = 90\%$$
$$\text{Sarah's overall repeatability} = 7/10 = 70\%$$

Calculating Precision: Reproducibility

Reproducibility is the variation that occurs when *two or more people* measure the *same unit* with the *same* measuring *device*. For discrete data, this is determined by the number of times all persons achieved the same result (percent agreement). In this case, the team asked two people from operations to review the same set of documents and record the number of errors per document. Table 2.7 shows the results.

Table 2.7 Reproducibility

Form Name	Data Collector 1	Data Collector 2	Match?
New Account	11	11	Y
Wire Transfer	13	11	N
Brokerage	12	12	Y
Car Application	10	10	Y
Home Equity Loan Application	15	15	Y
Compliance	1	2	N
Legal	1	1	Y
ACAT Form	5	5	Y
IRA Application	99	98	N
Business Account	0	0	Y

Based on the Lean Six Sigma team's findings, in three instances, the two team members' results did not match.

Reproducibility = agreement between operators/total units
Reproducibility = 7 / 10 = 70%

Putting the Whole Picture Together

To calculate the adequacy of the measurement system, we need to determine the overall repeatability, reproducibility, and accuracy (R&R&A), otherwise stated, *How many times overall did both operations people match themselves, each other, and the master in both trials?* Table 2.8 shows the results.

Table 2.8   Measurement Adequacy

Form Name	Master	Adam 1	Adam 2	Sarah 1	Sarah 2
New Account	11	11	(10)	11	11
Wire Transfer	13	13	13	13	13
Brokerage	12	12	12	12	12
Car Loan Application	10	10	10	10	(9)
Home Equity Loan Application	15	15	15	15	15
Compliance	1	1	1	1	(2)
Legal	1	1	1	1	1
ACAT Form	5	5	5	5	(3)
IRA Application	99	99	99	99	99
Business Account	0	0	0	0	0

In total, there are four instances in which Adam and Sarah don't match themselves, the master, or each other.

$$\text{Overall R\&R\&A} = 6/10 = 60\%$$

Is 60 percent measurement accuracy good enough? This means that every time someone records an error in a document, there is a 40 percent chance that the report is not correct. The general guideline is that there needs to be a 90 percent match.

Summary of Step 8: Validate the Measurement System

Process data will be the basis for the Lean Six Sigma team's analysis and its ultimate list of improvement recommendations. While this step is often overlooked, it is critical for the team to ensure that the data that are being collected and used for analysis are accurate and reliable. This means that the process and the system used to generate the data are adequate—the variability is understood, measured, and within tolerance. As previously stated, the risks of using data from a measurement system that has unacceptable levels of variability, which translates into poor accuracy, are that good services or products are rejected (a cost issue), or that bad services or products are accepted (a quality issue).

MEASURE PHASE SUMMARY

The journey of the Measure phase starts with the use of process mapping to better understand the process—it is all about uncovering the unknown or assumed. Documentation of the process will help uncover critical but missing data points. Once the process is better understood, then the team can start brainstorming possible points of risk by using a fishbone diagram or FMEA. These activities all lead to the identification of data that need to be collected in order to better understand the problem and its root causes in the Analyze phase. But before data can be analyzed, the team must first define a data collection plan that will ensure consistency and then test the measurement system to ensure accuracy. The Measure phase is the "feeder" to the problem-solving and solution-finding phases (Analyze and Improve). Poorly collected data or an inadequate process map will hinder all upcoming activities, leading to incorrect or suboptimal results.

MEASURE PHASE CHECKLIST

- ☑ Link the customer CTQ or need to a characteristic of the process or service.
- ☑ Ensure that your operational definition of CTQ performance is the same as the customer's.
- ☑ Define a defect, target performance, and upper and lower specification limits.
- ☑ Develop a data collection plan (if historical data are not available).
- ☑ Ensure that a reliable measurement system is in place.

QUESTIONS TO ASK AT THE END OF THE MEASURE PHASE

1. Which physical processes are targeted in this project?
2. Can the problem be tackled by a single project? Do we need to separate the CTQs?
3. Is the measurement continuous? Will it show the true level of variation?

4. Will the measurement reflect the customer's view of a single transaction?

5. What are the weaknesses of this measurement? How can it be manipulated?

APPLICATION OF LEAN SIX SIGMA CASE STUDY— MEASURE PHASE DELIVERABLES

The continuation of the case study illustrates the Measure phase of a Lean Six Sigma project.

Step 5: Define the CTQ Characteristics (Project Y)

With the approval from the Lean Six Sigma Steering Committee, the team can now proceed to the Measure phase. A detailed process map is created to ensure that everyone has a common understanding of the flow, key inputs, and deliverables. A segment of the map is shown in Figure 2.20.

Figure 2.20   Case Study Process Map

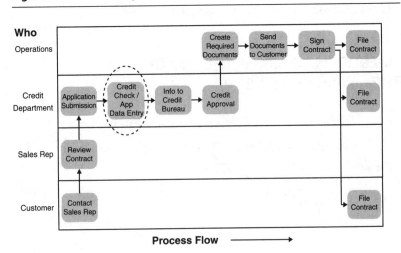

The map helps the team identify the process steps that have historically caused issues in approving loan applications. Using the fishbone tool (Figure 2.21), the team begins discussing the possible root causes of the issues that are leading to unacceptable response times. Armed with this information, the team now focuses its data collection and analysis efforts on a few key drivers.

Figure 2.21   Case Study Fishbone Diagram

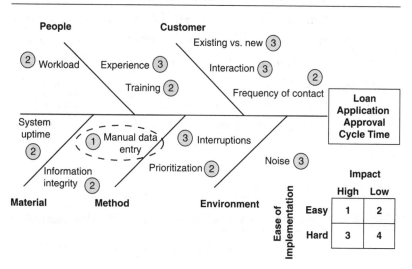

Step 6: Outline Performance Standard

The team has to determine the best way to measure the problem and also agree on a definition of a defect. Using interviews with customers and with key staff members in sales and operations, the team is able to define an upper specification, a lower specification, a target, and a defect definition (see Figure 2.22).

Steps 7 and 8: Develop a Data Collection Plan and Validate the Measurement System

The Lean Six Sigma team wanted to ensure that the complaints received by the sales team could be validated by data—that is, were the results really as bad as the customers were saying? However, to do this, the team needed to ensure that the data collection and measurement systems were adequate. Loan applications were either sent in electronically, in which case the system generated an automatic time stamp, or they were mailed in. The applications with system time stamps did not require further investigation—the second the loan officer pressed "submit application," the system would generate a time stamp. However, for the 30 percent of the applications that were received via mail, the application was scanned by the administrator and the application information was manually entered into the system. While it was impossible to determine the length of time that the application waited to be scanned, the team could determine the cycle time between scanning and data entry (which then would make the application available for operations to begin the review process).

Figure 2.22 Case Study Performance Standard

- 1,100 applications processed per month
- Customer expects fund delivery within 3 days (72 hours) of initial contact with loan officer
- Loan officer requires a minimum of 12 hours to review customer information, otherwise there is a high risk of making a "poor" decision about customer's eligibility
- Under stable conditions, an operations analyst can document a new loan in 24 hours

Upper Specification Limit:	3 days (72 hours)
Lower Specification Limit:	12 hours
Defect:	Beyond 3 days (72 hours) or before 12 hours
Target:	36 hours
Opportunities per Year:	1,100 × 12 months = 13,200

The team agreed that it should only take four minutes to enter data, and that anything beyond that could indicate a measurement system issue. Based on 250 data points, there were only four instances in which the system time stamp and the file time stamp did not meet the four-minute timeline (see Table 2.9). Therefore, the measurement system accuracy is around 98.4 percent $(1 - (4/250)) \times 100\%$. The team could, with confidence, rely on the historical data to provide a true depiction of process performance.

Table 2.9   Case Study Time Stamps

Time Stamps on File	Time Stamp in System	Calculated Difference (Min)
5:07	4:57	10
7:40	7:53	7
14:40	14:35	5
13:08	13:04	4
19:53	19:54	1
22:36	22:39	3
12:12	12:13	1
14:11	14:14	3
18:24	18:25	1
16:41	16:43	2
12:36	12:36	0
9:57	9:57	0
15:54	15:54	0
19:18	19:20	2
16:13	16:16	3

ANALYZE

y the time the team reaches the Analyze phase (see Figure 3.1), the business case for the project has been approved, potential resistance from key stakeholders has been reduced, the process has been mapped, and critical process data have been collected. The end goal of this phase is to take all the collected information and data and identify the root cause of the problem. The Analyze phase is divided into three steps:

Step 9: Baseline the process's current capability—how good is our process?

Step 10: Define the performance objectives for the process—how good do we need to be?

Step 11: Identify sources of variation—what are the key drivers of the problem

Figure 3.1   Overview of Analyze Phase

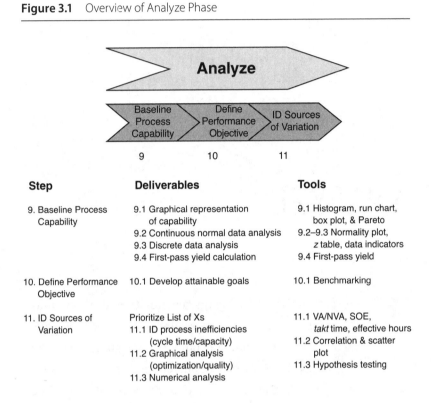

Step	Deliverables	Tools
9. Baseline Process Capability	9.1 Graphical representation of capability 9.2 Continuous normal data analysis 9.3 Discrete data analysis 9.4 First-pass yield calculation	9.1 Histogram, run chart, box plot, & Pareto 9.2–9.3 Normality plot, z table, data indicators 9.4 First-pass yield
10. Define Performance Objective	10.1 Develop attainable goals	10.1 Benchmarking
11. ID Sources of Variation	Prioritize List of Xs 11.1 ID process inefficiencies (cycle time/capacity) 11.2 Graphical analysis (optimization/quality) 11.3 Numerical analysis	11.1 VA/NVA, SOE, *takt* time, effective hours 11.2 Correlation & scatter plot 11.3 Hypothesis testing

The tools that we will use in the Analyze phase will be driven in large part by the goals of our project. If the focus is on improving cycle time, eliminating inventory, or standardizing a process, the team will rely more on the Lean tools and principles for analysis. If the focus is on improving the quality of a service, determining optimal pricing, or reducing losses, Six Sigma's analytical tools will be better suited. The project type drives the usage of the tools.

The key deliverables in this phase are:

- Determination of the data distribution type: normal or nonnormal
- The capability of the process: z score and DPMO
- Establish an improvement goal or performance objectives

- Determination of the stability, shape, center, and spread of the process
- Determination of the vital few Xs that affect the project Y
- Determination of which Lean tools to use to identify process bottlenecks
- Recommendations for the Improve phase

STEP 9: BASELINE THE PROCESS'S CURRENT CAPABILITY

Before we can investigate and identify the root cause of a problem, the capability of the process in its current state needs to be determined. This is primarily done to provide quantifiable evidence that when changes have been implemented (during the Improve phase), the results are positive. If we don't know how the process is performing in relation to customer expectations, how can we prove that the implemented changes have enhanced it?

The concept of capability is about measuring how a process performs in relation to a set of requirements. If our process cycle time to close a loan is 10 days, but the customer expects that loan within 7 days, how capable is this process? The metric that can help us define capability—that is, determine the performance of our process relative to customer needs and wants—is the z score. The z score is also known as the sigma score; the name Six Sigma is derived from this. The higher the sigma score, the more capable the performance of our process.

How to Start Baselining a Process

Baselining or understanding the performance of a process is done by first getting a graphical representation using the collected process data and then conducting statistical analysis.

Baselining Process Capability—Graphical Method

There are several tools available for getting a graphical representation of a process:

1. Histogram
2. Run chart
3. Box plot
4. Pareto analysis

Why do we start with a graph rather than jumping into the numerical analysis? A graph or a picture allows you to become familiar with the process in a way that numerical analysis cannot: it provides a pictorial representation of trends and anomalies in the process. Anomalies and unexpected trends in the data should be investigated and resolved prior to further analysis. Statistical software that is used to analyze data inherently assumes that the data are well understood and accurate. In short, the results derived from numerical analysis are only as good as the data. The additional benefits of a graph and/or pictorial representation of data are that they facilitate sharing and communicating findings with the champion and key stakeholders.

Histogram

A histogram provides information about the shape, central tendency, and variability of a process. It is most often used to determine whether:

1. The process is on target and meeting customer requirements.
2. The variation in a process is normal or whether something has caused the process to vary in an unusual way.

The main benefits of a histogram are:

1. It displays variation in a process.

2. It converts an unorganized set of data or group of measurements into a coherent picture.

Figure 3.2 shows a histogram on loan closure cycle time.

Figure 3.2   Histogram

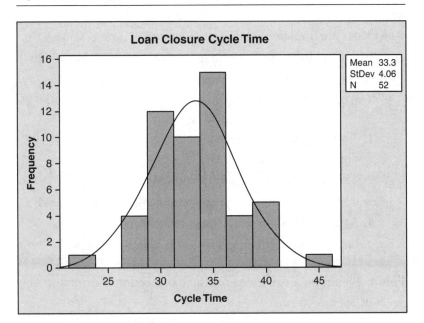

Here's how to interpret the graph: The central tendency (average or mean) of the process is 33.3 days. Based on the bars on the graph, a loan can be closed in anywhere from 22 days to 45 days. The team can use the graph to pursue three ideas:

1. Is the range of loan closure (22 to 45 days) acceptable?
2. Is an average response time of 33 days acceptable?

3. There seem to be two potential anomalies in the data: loans
   closed in less than 25 days and loans closed after 40 days.
   Further investigation may be required to ensure that the
   data were collected properly. If our data are reliable, we
   need to determine why these two outliers occurred.

Run Chart

Run charts are used to track the performance of a process over time
and display trends in the performance of that process. They help to
focus attention on changes in the process.

The benefits of run charts are:

1. They help establish a baseline of performance as a starting
   point for improvement.
2. They uncover changes in the process.
3. They enable you to brainstorm possible causes for trends.
4. After the Improve phase, they can help you compare the
   historical performance of a process with the improved one.

Figure 3.3 shows a run chart for the daily count of errors on new
account opening forms.

Here's how to interpret the graph: For the first 6 days, the total
error count is approximately 32; however, there seems to be a process
shift around the fifteenth day, and the error count begins to increase
steadily. This change in the process needs investigation. In order to
continue, we need to determine the root cause of the shift and whether
the entire data set should be used for numerical analysis. If a change
that caused the shift in performance was implemented on the twentieth
day, should we include the data before that date for analysis? Or should
we separate the data, since we are looking at two different versions
of the same process? The answers to these questions help the team
determine how to conduct numerical analysis.

Figure 3.3 Run Chart

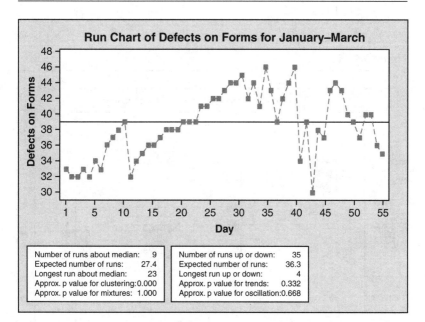

Source: Minitab Inc. Printed with permission of Minitab Inc. This figure remains the exclusive property and copyright of Minitab Inc. All rights reserved.

Box Plot

A box plot is an ideal tool for comparing the distribution of multiple processes.

In Figure 3.4, the cycle time for new account opening in four regions is being compared. Which region is performing best? San Francisco. The discussion of how to interpret the graph will explain the reasoning.

Here's how to interpret the graph: The box plot helps describe the process using six different data points:

1. Minimum value observed
2. Maximum value observed
3. Twenty-fifth percentile
4. Median (fiftieth percentile)

5. Seventy-fifth percentile

6. Outliers

Figure 3.4 Box Plot

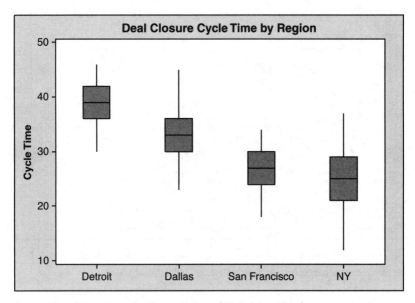

The length of the box, which is determined by the distance between the twenty-fifth and seventy-fifth percentiles of the data set, indicates the level of variation or spread in the process (the smaller the size of the box, the less the variation). The horizontal line inside the box shows the median, or the middle point in the data set (the closer that line is to the desired value, the better). Figure 3.5 shows the details of a box's construction.

When comparing the cycle times of the four regions, which can we say is performing best? San Francisco; the length of its box compared to the others is the smallest (lowest amount of variation), and it has the second lowest median (New York has the lowest cycle

Figure 3.5 Box Plot Construction

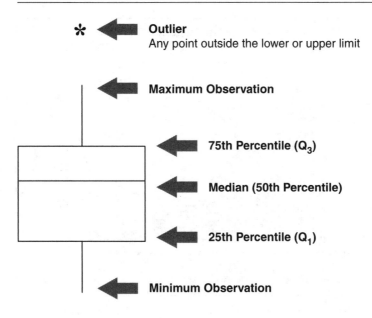

time median, but a larger amount of variation). Stated in numerical terms, the San Francisco office's typical response time is 26 days.

Pareto Analysis

Pareto analysis is used to separate the vital few causes (X) from the trivial many by comparing the frequency of occurrence. Project leaders can use this tool to help them select areas on which to focus.

Figure 3.6 shows a Pareto chart of customer feedback. A bank conducted a survey to better understand why loan applicants did not select it as the primary lender.

Here's how to interpret the graph: Based on voice of the customer (VOC), the three top reasons for customers not selecting the bank are price, delivery time, and overall speed of execution. Based on the row labeled "count," price was noted by the customers 45 times, delivery

Figure 3.6   Pareto Chart

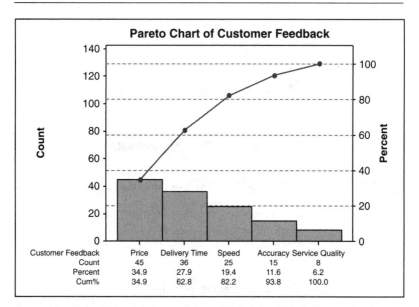

time 36 times, and speed 25 times. The row labeled Cum% calculates the cumulative percentage effect—if we were to address the top three reasons, 82 percent of complaints would be resolved.

Baselining Process Capability—Numerical Method

The goal of this step is to calculate what is called a z score, also known as the sigma score. The z score is a statistical representation of capability. It is a measure of a process's ability to meet customer expectations: by comparing the variation within the process to the customer's tolerance, we can determine capability. For example, we know that a bank's customers expect to receive their checkbooks within 30 days of opening an account. Any checkbook received after 30 days is deemed a defect or unacceptable. The average cycle time for the process is 26 days with a standard deviation of 4 days (see Figure 3.7). How capable is this process? The *z* score helps relate the mean and standard deviation to the customer's expectation, resulting in a capability metric.

Figure 3.7 Expectation

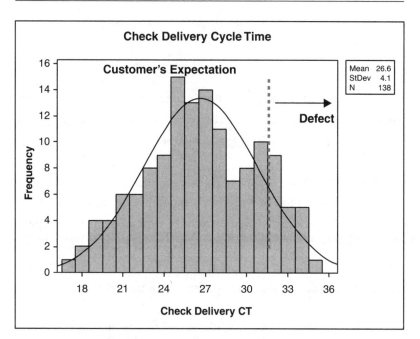

Source: Minitab Inc. Printed with permission of Minitab Inc. This figure remains the exclusive property and copyright of Minitab Inc. All rights reserved.

Why calculate a *z* score?

The *z* score creates a standard metric for measuring process capability. This allows processes across the organization to be compared. To make the case, which of the processes in Table 3.1 is performing better: account opening with an average cycle time of 30 minutes ± 5 minutes or the billing process with 95 percent accuracy ± 1 percent?

Table 3.1   Current Performance

Process	Current Performance
Account opening cycle time	30 ± 5 minutes average account opening time
Billing	$95 \pm 1\%$ accuracy
Accounts receivable	65 ± 5 days average aging
Client experience	85% rated 4 or 5 on service level

It is difficult to compare processes that are measured differently. However, a z score can be calculated for each of these processes, creating a standard platform for comparison.

Calculating the Z Score

Numerical calculation of a process's capability depends on two factors: the shape of the distribution and the type of data. The shape of the distribution determines whether the data are normally distributed or the distribution has a different shape. The data type determines whether the collected data are continuous or discrete.

What Is the Difference Between Continuous and Discrete Data?   By definition, with continuous data, there is an infinite number of possible values. Furthermore, the data can always be subdivided into smaller values. Examples are claim amount, cycle time, and loan amount. Discrete data, on the other hand, have finite values. Examples are pass/fail, good/bad, and percent rejected.

It is always advisable to collect continuous data for Lean Six Sigma projects. Continuous data provide two types of information about the process: frequency and magnitude. If we collect discrete data for new account opening cycle time, we will know only whether the account was opened on time or late. For cases in which it was opened late, we will not know by how much, and thus we will not be able to discuss the severity of the impact.

How Do I Know if I Have Normal Process Data?   Normal data sets, when plotted, have the shape of a bell curve. However, the easiest way to conduct a normality test is by using a statistical software package. The one most often used for Lean Six Sigma projects is Minitab. The normality test will help determine whether the distribution of the data is normal. Figure 3.8 shows what the different distributions look like.

Figure 3.8   Distribution Types

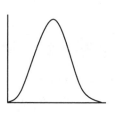 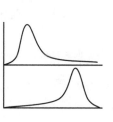

Normal   **Skewed**   **Long-tailed**

Most often, transaction-based processes are not normally distributed, but are either skewed or long-tailed. Process cycle time data are most often long-tailed—we have accounts that were opened either earlier than expected or much later than expected. Claims submitted by owners are most often skewed in shape depending on the claim type. Your process data distribution directly affects the type of analysis you can use.

Z Score for Normal Continuous Data

The following is the mathematical equation for calculating the z score:

$$z \text{ score} = (\text{process average} - \text{customer specification limit})/ \text{process standard deviation}^*$$

Here is an example to demonstrate the usage and interpretation of the equation. A Lean Six Sigma team collected one month of cycle time data for wire transfer requests. The customer's expectation is to have the wire transfer completed within 5 days of the request. The bank's average cycle time for the wire transfer is 3 days with a standard deviation of 1.5 day. (Note: the average and standard deviation values can be calculated using either Excel functions or statistical software.)

$$z \text{ score} = (5 - 3)/1.5 = 1.3$$

Using Table 3.2, the team determines that the process sigma (z score) of 1.3 translates to 570,000 defects per million opportunities. Or using the yield column the probability of getting the wire out within the customer-requested timeline is 43 percent.

Z Score for Discrete and Nonnormal Data

If the process output or collected data are discrete, then a defects per million opportunities (DPMO) number should be calculated. The DPMO number can be converted to a z score using Table 3.2.

---

*Standard deviation is a measure of variability. The larger the value of the standard deviation, the greater the process variation. A low standard deviation indicates that data points collected from the process are all very close in value to the average, which indicates low levels of process variation.

Table 3.2 Process Sigma

Yield	Process Sigma(ST)	Defects per 1,000,000	Yield	Process Sigma(ST)	Defects per 1,000,000
99.99966%	6.0	3.4	90.320%	2.8	96,800
99.9995%	5.9	5	88.50%	2.7	115,000
99.9992%	5.8	8	86.50%	2.6	135,000
99.9990%	5.7	10	84.20%	2.5	158,000
99.9980%	5.6	20	81.60%	2.4	184,000
99.9970%	5.5	30	78.80%	2.3	212,000
99.9960%	5.4	40	75.80%	2.2	242,000
99.9930%	5.3	70	72.60%	2.1	274,000
99.9900%	5.2	100	69.20%	2.0	308,000
99.9850%	5.1	150	65.60%	1.9	344,000
99.9770%	5.0	230	61.80%	1.8	382,000
99.9670%	4.9	330	58.00%	1.7	420,000
99.9520%	4.8	480	54.00%	1.6	460,000
99.9320%	4.7	680	50%	1.5	500,000
99.9040%	4.6	960	46%	1.4	540,000
99.8650%	4.5	1,350	43%	1.3	570,000
99.8140%	4.4	1,860	39%	1.2	610,000
99.7450%	4.3	2,550	35%	1.1	650,000
99.6540%	4.2	3,460	31%	1.0	690,000
99.5340%	4.1	4,660	28%	0.9	720,000
99.3790%	4.0	6,210	25%	0.8	750,000
99.1810%	3.9	8,190	22%	0.7	780,000
98.930%	3.8	10,700	19%	0.6	810,000
98.610%	3.7	13,900	16%	0.5	840,000
98.220%	3.6	17,800	14%	0.4	860,000
97.730%	3.5	22.700	12%	0.3	880,000
97.130%	3.4	28,700	10%	0.2	900,000
96.410%	3.3	35,900	8%	0.1	920,000
95.540%	3.2	44,600			
94.520%	3.1	54,800			
93.320%	3.0	66,800			
91.920%	2.9	80,800			

In order to calculate a DPMO, three pieces of information are needed: the number of units being inspected or audited, the number of opportunities for error per unit, and a count of defects.

DPMO = (total defects/total opportunities) $\times$ 1,000,000
= [(total count of defects)/(number of units $\times$ number of opportunities per unit)] $\times$ 1,000,000

A *unit* is anything that is to be inspected or reviewed in order to ensure that it meets the customer's specifications—for example, an application, a claim, or an incoming call.

An *opportunity* is the characteristic or requirement that is being inspected. If it is missed or incorrect, it will lead to customer dissatisfaction—for example, the fields or questions on a loan application or the types of images required from a CT scan.

A *defect* is anything that results in customer dissatisfaction—for example, data fields missed on an application.

Here is an example to demonstrate the usage and interpretation of the equation. The focus of a Lean Six Sigma project is to improve account opening accuracy. The measure is the completeness of the application. Each application has 21 required fields (*opportunities*). You have defined any required field that is not completed as a defect. To get your baseline data, you collect a sample of 200 applications (*units*). After reviewing each application, you count a total of 30 *defects*.

DPMO = [(30)/(200 $\times$ 21)] $\times$ 1,000,000 = 7,143

Using the conversion table (Table 3.2), a DPMO of 7,143 roughly translates to a *z* score of 3.95.

But what does all this mean?

What is a *z* score of 2 or 3.8 or 6? What is the practical translation of this number?

If a process has a *z* score of 2, this implies that you are looking at a two sigma process. And a sigma or *z* score can always be translated to a DPMO number (how many errors a process can expect given a million opportunities). On a practical level, the higher the *z* score, the higher the capability of the process: it has a lower chance of producing an error and thus causing customer dissatisfaction. By the time a process has reached a *z* score of 6, otherwise stated as a six sigma process, it produces only 3.4 errors per million opportunities.

In statistical terms, a *z* score of 3 posits that three units of standard deviation can fit between the average performance of a process (μ) and the customer's expectation (upper specification level, or USL). Standard deviation (σ) is a measure of variability. The less variation a process experiences, the more stable the process and so the smaller its standard deviation value. Otherwise stated, the bell curve shape of processes with low standard deviation is very tight and narrow (see Figure 3.9).

Figure 3.9   Bell Curves with Big and Small Standard Deviation

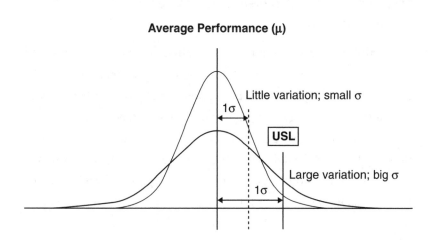

The smaller the standard deviation value, the more units can be fitted between the mean and the specification limit. So it follows that the more units of variation we can fit between the mean and the specification limit, the more capable the process (see Figure 3.10).

Figure 3.10   Three and Six Sigma Processes

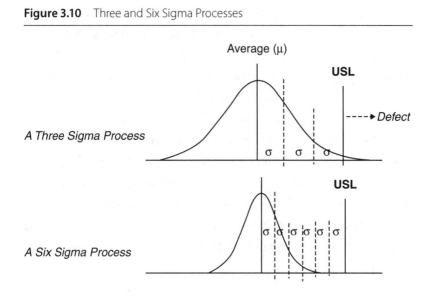

Summary of Step 9: Baseline the Process's Current Capability

The main deliverable of Step 9 is a baseline of the current capability of the process that is in need of improvement. The team needs to be able to answer the question, "How good is our process?" In order to provide an answer, first the project leader has to have a better understanding of the process data that have been collected: Were there any trends in the data? Had the process experienced a shift? If so, were the reasons known? Is one region performing better than another? Once the process has been better understood, a capability score known as the z score needs to be calculated for the process.

STEP 10: DEFINE THE PERFORMANCE OBJECTIVE FOR THE PROCESS

Defining the performance objective (see Figure 3.11) helps answer the question, "How good do we need to be?" While a goal or target for the project was stated in the Define phase, at this point it can be further refined. The combination of the following elements (see Figure 3.12) can help us with goal refinement:

- Benchmarking a best-in-class process
- Understanding process entitlement
- Understanding the current process capability

Figure 3.11   Analyze Phase Step 10

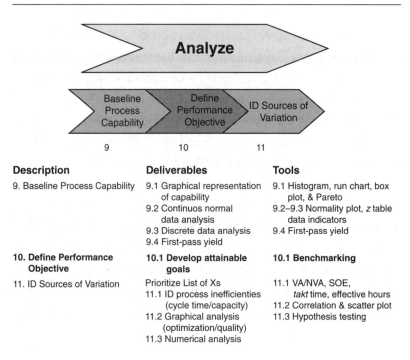

Description	Deliverables	Tools
9. Baseline Process Capability	9.1 Graphical representation of capability 9.2 Continuos normal data analysis 9.3 Discrete data analysis 9.4 First-pass yield	9.1 Histogram, run chart, box plot, & Pareto 9.2–9.3 Normality plot, z table data indicators 9.4 First-pass yield
10. Define Performance Objective	**10.1 Develop attainable goals**	**10.1 Benchmarking**
11. ID Sources of Variation	Prioritize List of Xs 11.1 ID process inefficienties (cycle time/capacity) 11.2 Graphical analysis (optimization/quality) 11.3 Numerical analysis	11.1 VA/NVA, SOE, *takt* time, effective hours 11.2 Correlation & scatter plot 11.3 Hypothesis testing

Figure 3.12   Benchmarking

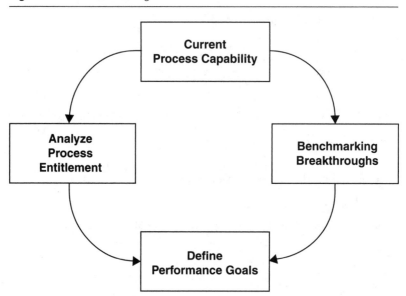

Process entitlement can be understood by analyzing the historical performance of a process. Entitlement denotes the best the process can perform given today's constraints, whether they be technology, human capital, or regulatory constraints. As an example, if the objective of a project is to reduce process cycle time, several months of process data can be graphed using a trend chart. This chart can help determine whether there was a point in time at which the process performed better than at other times. For the example provided in Figure 3.13, between fiscal weeks 8 and 14, the process cycle time was consistently below the average time of 10 days. This period can be considered the entitlement level for the process—the best it can perform without any significant investment or changes.

Using best-in-class benchmarking in conjunction with process entitlement can help to further refine the target. The main benefit of

Figure 3.13   Process Entitlement

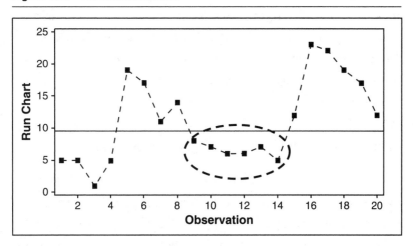

benchmarking is that it provides a platform that enables the team to compare the process's internal practices to those of processes with superior performance. Benchmarking of a best-in-class process can be done internally or externally. Identifying a functional area or business unit internal to the company that is performing well makes benchmarking a relatively easy task:

- Data can be easily collected and shared.
- Technology and policies should be similar.
- There is a common corporate culture.

Alternatively, benchmarking a competitor or companies in similar industries who have similar operating characteristics has high potential for discovery and may lead to outside-the-box thinking.

The combination of baselining capability with either benchmarking and/or identifying process entitlement can help in refining the project goal—it can ensure that the target is attainable. In the end, regardless of the approach that the team has taken to determine the project goal, one thing remains constant: the customer has to recognize the improvement.

STEP 11: IDENTIFY SOURCES OF VARIATION

Up to this point, there has been very little distinction between the Lean and Six Sigma methodologies. However in this step, the tool selection will rely heavily on the project deliverables (see Figure 3.14). If the project is focused on standardization, stabilization of a process (has a z score

Figure 3.14   Analyze Phase Step 11

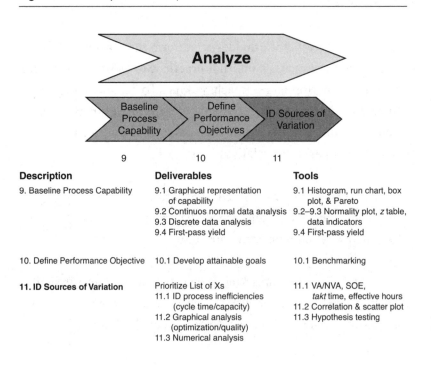

Description	Deliverables	Tools
9. Baseline Process Capability	9.1 Graphical representation of capability	9.1 Histogram, run chart, box plot, & Pareto
	9.2 Continuos normal data analysis	9.2–9.3 Normality plot, z table, data indicators
	9.3 Discrete data analysis	
	9.4 First-pass yield	9.4 First-pass yield
10. Define Performance Objective	10.1 Develop attainable goals	10.1 Benchmarking
11. ID Sources of Variation	Prioritize List of Xs	11.1 VA/NVA, SOE,
	11.1 ID process inefficiencies (cycle time/capacity)	*takt* time, effective hours
	11.2 Graphical analysis (optimization/quality)	11.2 Correlation & scatter plot
	11.3 Numerical analysis	11.3 Hypothesis testing

of <1), or reduction in cycle time, there will be a heavier focus on the Lean tools. On the other hand, if the *z* score of the process is >3, and data are required to uncover the root cause of the issue, then Six Sigma tools are more appropriate (see Figure 3.15).

Figure 3.15   Lean vs. Six Sigma

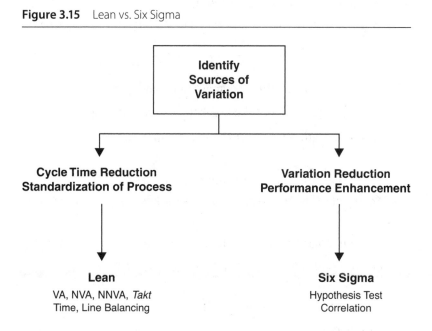

How will Lean tools help to identify sources of variation? The two focal points of Lean tools are:

1. To ensure that the product, service, or information flows seamlessly through its various transformations until it reaches the customer.
2. To ensure that all waste in the process has been identified and eliminated. This ensures that all process steps add value from a customer's perspective.

A process step adds value only if it changes the form, fit, or function of the product or service that is being delivered. When it does so, the customer, by definition, is willing to pay for the process step. Any process step that adds only cost and/or time is considered waste. Reduction of waste shrinks the cycle time of a process, making it more reliable and reducing variability.

It is critical to note that all businesses have three main value streams:

1. From initial customer contact to receiving an "order"
2. From the receipt of the order to customer delivery
3. From customer delivery to the receipt of cash

When you are working on a project that will utilize Lean tools, it is important to ensure that the scope is limited to one of these main value streams.

If Lean tools will be applied, the success of the team in identifying and eliminating variation can be gauged by its having:

- Reduced work-in-process (WIP), otherwise known as backlog or inventory.
- Increased productivity and capacity (doing more with the same amount of resources or less).
- Standardized the process or operation.

The two main Lean tools available to accomplish these goals are:

1. Value-Add, Necessary Non-Value-Add, and Non-Value-Add analysis
2. *Takt* Time study

Identifying Sources of Variation: Value-Add, Necessary-Non-Value-Add, and Non-Value-Add Analysis

When the goal is reducing process cycle time, standardization, or stabilization, a value-add (VA), non-value-add (NVA), necessary-non-value-add (NNVA) study helps assess the true value of each process step from the customer's perspective. Here are the required definitions for this study:

Value-Add. Activities that are critical, as they change the form, fit, or function of the service and/or product. If they are performed correctly, the customer is willing to pay for them.

Necessary Non-Value-Add. While these activities don't add value to the product or service, they are necessary in order to complete the process. Examples include compliance audits and imaging documents.

Non-Value-Add. These steps are pure waste. Most often these steps have been added to the process over time to compensate for process, technology and/or employee shortcomings. There are seven types of waste to consider. These are described in Table 3.3.

The main purposes of this study are:

- To drive productivity by minimizing and eliminating NVA
- To identify opportunities for automation or elimination
- To minimize the hold, wait, and/or transfer time in a process

How to Use This Tool

Starting with the process map that was developed in the Measure phase, the team members should review each step. Through discussion, they

Table 3.3   Seven Types of Waste

Type of Waste	Description
Defects	Any nonconformance that leads to redoing, reworking, recontacting, or reviewing. Examples include missing critical data on forms and not sending out a debit card in time.
Waiting	Any time during which work not being performed on the customer request. Examples include waiting for approval and waiting for branch feedback.
Overproduction	Producing more than required or more than a process step has the capacity to handle, resulting in the building of inventory. An example is batch processing of applications.
Unnecessary transportation	Movement of files, data, or customer requests. With every movement, there is a risk of loss or delays in processing.
Inventory	Work-in-process, representing unrecognized potential revenue. An example is applications waiting for processing.
Overprocessing	Doing more than is required from a customer's perspective.
Motion	Movement to transport information or data. An example is extra steps taken by employees to accommodate an inefficient process layout.

are to assess whether each step is NVA, VA, or NNVA. For all NVA and NNVA steps, they need to develop and implement a list of recommendations for elimination or reduction.

Figure 3.16 is an example of this analysis for a wire transfer process in a brokerage firm. Once the process had been mapped, a cross-functional team assessed the value of each step. Later on, in the Improve phase, the process was reengineered, eliminating steps where possible, simplifying the process, and reducing the probability of making errors.

Figure 3.16 VA/NVA Analysis

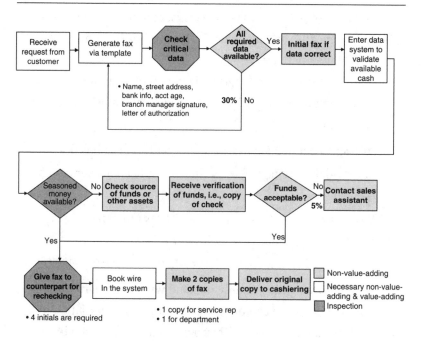

Takt Time Analysis

Takt Time analysis is another powerful Lean tool that is most often used in the Analyze phase. *Takt* time, otherwise known as operational cycle time, is the targeted rate at which requests or services need to be completed in order to meet customer demand. It is the drumbeat of a process. Examples of *takt* time include an application correctly entered into the system every 5 minutes, a loan underwriting completed every 30 minutes, and a quote completed every 3 hours. Mathematically, *takt* time is calculated as:

$$Takt = (\text{effective hours} \times \text{\# of shifts})/\text{demand}$$

Effective hours. The number of hours an employee actually works, that is, subtracting breaks, meetings, and lunch from an 8-hour day. Typically, an employee's effective hours are between 6.5 and 7 hours per day

Demand. The maximum targeted daily output. This number should include expected growth. Here is an example of how to calculate daily demand:

Average incoming applications	= 1,500 applications per month
Standard deviation	= 50 applications per month
Growth	= 20%
Work days	= 20 days/month
Monthly production	= $X + 3 \times$ st. dev.
	= 1,500 + 3 × 50 = 1,650

By multiplying the monthly demand with 3 standard deviation, we ensure that we have captured 99.99% of possible variation in the process. While it builds some overcapacity in the process, it will ensure that the organization can consistently meet customer demand regardless of incoming volume.

$$\text{Demand} = \frac{1,650 \text{ applications} / \text{month} \times 120\% \text{ (growth)}}{20 \text{ days} / \text{month}}$$

Demand = 99 applications / day

You will notice that in the calculation of demand, both growth and standard deviation were used. This ensures that the process will be able to handle both growth and the normal oscillation in daily demand.

Given the effective hours and expected demand, the drumbeat of the process, *takt* time, can be calculated.

Takt = 6.5 hr × 60 min/99 applications = 4 min

This indicates that in order to keep up with customer demand (not allowing the buildup of backlog), an application must be completed every 4 minutes.

How to Use *Takt* Time Once It Is Calculated

Takt time has two main purposes:

1. Given a process cycle time, it can help calculate the required amount of resources.
2. It can help identify process bottlenecks.

Now that it has been determined that every step in processing an application needs to be completed—from start to finish—every 4 minutes, we can determine whether all process steps are capable of handling this requirement. By reviewing the cycle time of each process step required to complete an application, we can quickly determine which steps, if any, exceed the 4-minute ceiling we have calculated (see Figure 3.17). Any process step that requires more than 4 minutes will create an imbalance in the line.

If the cycle time for a particular process is 40 minutes, how many employees are needed?

$$\# \text{ of workers} = \frac{40 \text{ minutes (total process cycle time)}}{4 \text{ minutes } (\textit{takt} \text{ time})}$$

$$\# \text{ of workers} = 10$$

Figure 3.17 *Takt* Time

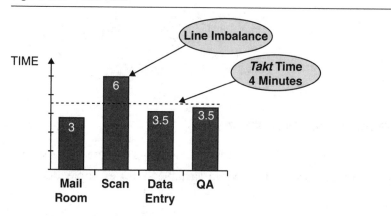

If you actually have 12 workers assigned to that process, this means that you have the opportunity to redesign the process and redeploy 2 workers to other parts of the business.

Identifying and verifying process variables that affect the overall performance of a process is not always easy. Statistical, graphical, and numerical analysis tools (see Figure 3.18) can help the team better understand where it needs to focus its energy.

Figure 3.18   Tools for Analyzing Process Performance

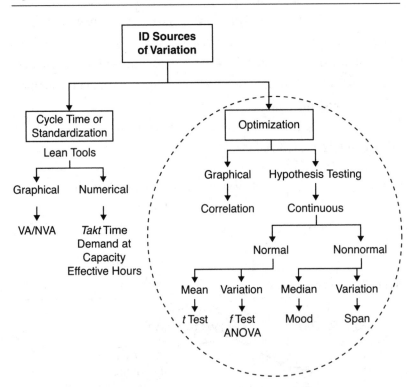

Graphical Tool: Correlation

A correlation study (linear dependence) helps explore the possibility of a relationship between two variables—for example, does the interest rate affect the number of refinancing applications? There are several types of relationships that can be identified: positive or negative, strong or weak, linear or nonlinear. The way to determine the relationship is by calculating a correlation coefficient, or r value. The correlation coefficient (also known as the Pearson correlation coefficient) determines the extent to which the values of two variables are proportional to each other. The r value can range from -1 to 1.

When

$r = 0$	There is no relationship.
$r = -1$	There is a strong negative relationship.
$r = +1$	There is a strong positive relationship.

Any r value less than 0.25 or greater than -0.25 is not significant. Figure 3.19 gives some examples of correlation.

Figure 3.19   Correlation

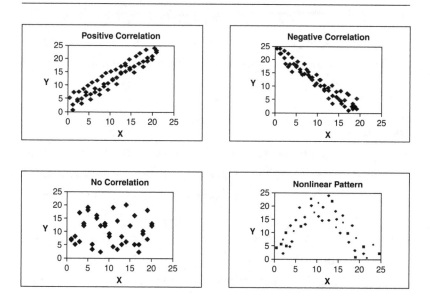

Warning!

1. **Correlation does not always imply causation.** Suppose
   we collected the average shoe size for citizens of several
   counties and then compared them to the average rainfall
   in those counties. If we got a possible correlation, would
   that mean that shoe size drives rainfall? The validity of
   the results from any statistical tool is dependent on the
   Black Belt or Green Belt. The knowledge of the process,
   products, or customer will ensure that the appropriate
   data are being considered for correlation.

2. **Absence of correlation does not mean lack of causation.**
   If the data do not seem to have a relationship, consider the
   following:

   - Did we collect data for a long enough time period?
   - Did we consider the entire process or just a portion of
     it—for example, the cycle time for the entire process or
     just the application entry?
   - Are the data a result of multiple processes, and do we
     need to consider them separately? (For example, does
     the morning shift operate differently from the afternoon
     shift?)

Practical Application

At a plant, the team was trying to determine whether response time
for providing a quote to the customer (cycle time) was affecting the
volume of goods sold. For five months the team members collected
data on the average cycle time and number of lost deals (canceled
orders). The correlation study yielded an r value of 0.97 and the graph
shown in Figure 3.20.

This strong linear relationship indicates that as cycle time increases,
so does the number of lost deals.

Figure 3.20   Correlation Study

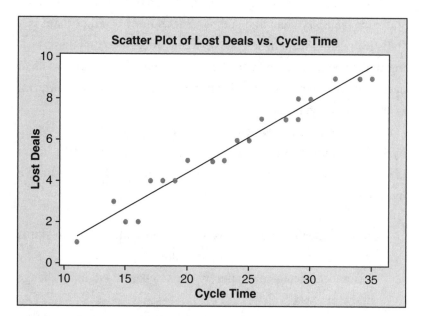

In summary, correlation study provides a good indication of whether process inputs actually affect the process output. Correlation is a measure of the relationship between two or more variables: the closer to +1 or −1 the r value, the stronger the relationship. What is a good r value? It all depends on the situation and the industry. In the biomedical industry, a new vaccine seeking FDA approval may need r values that are very close to 1, but in the banking sector, a project focused on accurate prediction of loan loss reserves may be happy with an r value of 0.7.

Hypothesis Testing

Hypothesis testing, a statistical tool, allows the comparison of two or more process attributes—mean, median, and standard deviation. It provides an objective method for determining differences. Sometimes we cannot decide through graphical methods or by using calculated statistics (sample mean and standard deviation) whether there is a statistically significant difference between processes. Hypothesis testing will provide that confirmation. In the end, this test allows us to determine whether observed differences are statistically significant or the result of chance.

A hypothesis is a statement of an assumption. You can state a hypothesis about anything. However, for hypothesis testing, there is a testing protocol: you need to have a null and an alternative hypothesis.

Null hypothesis (H_0). This is a statement validating the status quo—there will be *no* change of significance observed. Any differences detected are purely due to chance and not a change in the process.

Alternative hypothesis (H_a). This is a statement that there *will* be a difference of statistical significance detected.

Just remember that with any statistical test, we are making inferences about the population based on only a sample from that population. Thus, there is always a probability that we will come to an incorrect conclusion. Most statistical tests are run with a 95 percent confidence level, indicating that there is a 5 percent chance of making an error.

The decision of whether to accept or reject the null hypothesis is based on the calculated p value. If the p value is less than or equal to a preassigned significance level (normally set at 5 percent), then we reject the null hypothesis and accept the alternative. Otherwise stated, *if the* p *is low, the null must go!* A p value will be calculated by the statistical software when running a hypothesis test.

Types of Hypothesis Testing

Depending on the type of data you have and whether they are normal or nonnormal, there are several hypothesis tests available for comparing process characteristics (see Figure 3.21).

Figure 3.21   Types of Hypothesis Tests

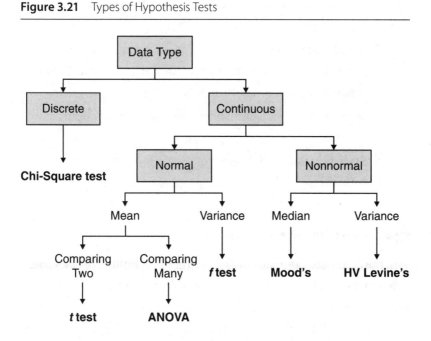

Hypothesis-Testing Process

In general, the following steps are followed when hypothesis testing is used:

1. The hypotheses are always statements about the population parameters. First, determine what you are trying to compare or detect a difference in—that is, central tendency (mean or median), variation, or proportion.

2. Set your H_0 and H_a; for example:

   H_0: The loan application data entry process of Commercial Loan Company is the same as those of its competitors.

   H_a: The loan application data entry process of Commercial Loan Company is longer than those of its competitors.

3. Remember that data type (normal or nonnormal) plays a key role in determining the type of test you select. So run a normality test to confirm data type.

4. Run the test using statistical software to generate the p value.

5. Based on the results, reject or fail to reject the null hypothesis.

Hypothesis Testing—Practical Application

A manufacturing company was hearing complaints from its sales reps about the delivery cycle time for one of its products (Product A). They claimed that the company's performance was affecting their relationship with their clients and hence the probability of selling them more products in the future. To validate their concerns, a Lean Six Sigma team decided to compare the delivery cycle time (order entry to actual ship date) for this one product to that for another high-volume one (Product B). The team members collected historical data for six months. The question at hand was: does Product A take longer to deliver than Product B?

The team ran a normality test and confirmed that both data sets were normal, thus, it selected a t test to compare the average delivery time for products A and B.

$$H_0: \mu_A = \mu_B$$

Null hypothesis: average delivery cycle time of Product A = average delivery cycle time of Product B.

$$H_a: \mu_A \neq \mu_B$$

Alternative hypothesis: average delivery cycle time of Product A ≠ average delivery cycle time of Product B.

Using statistical software, the test is run, and the following numerical results and graph are generated:

Two-sample t for Product A vs. Product B

	Mean
Product A	40.5
Product B	33.3

Difference = μ (Product A) − μ (Product B)
Estimate for difference = 7.16
95% confidence interval for difference = (4.05, 10.28)
p value = 0.000

With a p value < 0.05, we can reject the null hypothesis (and accept the alternative). There is a statistical difference between the delivery cycle time for Product A and that for Product B. The difference detected is 7.16 days. On average, Product A is delivered in 40.5 days, whereas Product B is delivered in 33.3 days. With the statistical confirmation, the team can use the correlation study to determine whether the longer cycle time is truly affecting sales volume.

These differences are highlighted in the box plots in Figure 3.22.

Figure 3.22 Case Study Box Plot

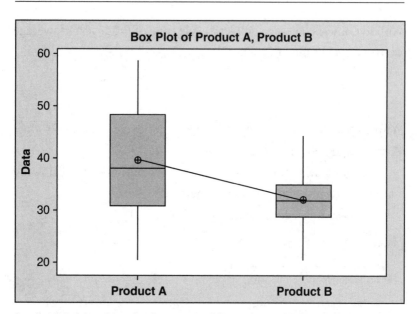

ANALYZE PHASE SUMMARY

The purpose of this phase is to start exploring all the possible root causes that can affect the performance of your process and/or your product. However, by the end of this phase, there should be only a short list of critical factors that need to be improved in order to meet the project goals. Graphical tools like the box plot, run chart, and histogram are great ways to develop a picture of your process's performance; this helps you detect patterns and potential outliers. Statistical tools like hypothesis testing can help ensure that observed differences in the process are statistically valid (not just based on chance). Lean tools, on the other hand, in the Analyze phase help the team focus on the root causes of service delays or inconsistencies by identifying non-value-adding activities and calculating *takt* time (the required production drumbeat to meet customer demand consistently).

This phase ends with the team members prioritizing their list of improvement opportunities and getting buy-in from the project champion and the process owners to move into the Improve phase.

ANALYZE PHASE CHECKLIST

- ☑ Develop a graphical representation of data to detect patterns.
- ☑ Define and calculate a z score or DPMO.
- ☑ Identify a list of potential Xs.
- ☑ Benchmark best-in-class operations to better refine the project goal.
- ☑ Do statistical testing on population differences.

QUESTIONS TO ASK AT THE END OF THE ANALYZE PHASE

1. What is the capability of the current process?
2. Is the process stable? Are your data normal?
3. Are the data discrete or continuous?
   - What does the distribution look like?
   - Has this helped you reduce the *potential Xs*?
4. Can you separate the vital few from the trivial many special causes?
5. What is the null hypothesis, and what is the alternate hypothesis? What is the conclusion of the analysis?
6. Do you have adequate resources to complete the project?
7. What are your next steps?

APPLICATION OF LEAN SIX SIGMA CASE STUDY— ANALYZE PHASE DELIVERABLES

The continuation of the case study illustrates the Analyze phase of a Lean Six Sigma project.

Step 9: Baseline the Process's Current Capability

The members of the project team calculated the process capability to ensure that they had properly documented the current performance level before any improvements were implemented. Using data for the previous year, they calculated the difference between the time when the borrower information packet was received and the time when a final decision was communicated to the borrower. Using statistical software (or Excel), they calculated the values for the average and standard deviation. Since they knew that the customer expects an answer within 3 days (72 hours), a z score was calculated:

> Average response time = 64 hours
> Standard deviation of response time = 27 hours
>
> z = (upper specification limit − average)/standard deviation
> = (72 hours − 64 hours)/27 hours
> = 0.3

The sigma value or z score of this process is 0.3, or less than 1. This is a very poorly performing process. The histogram in Figure 3.23 compares the current performance of the process with customer expectation (upper specification level) and the performance level required (target) in order to consistently meet customers' needs.

Step 10: Define the Performance Objectives for the Process

For this project, since the customer requirements were defined very clearly, benchmarking to refine the project goals was not required.

Figure 3.23   Case Study Histogram

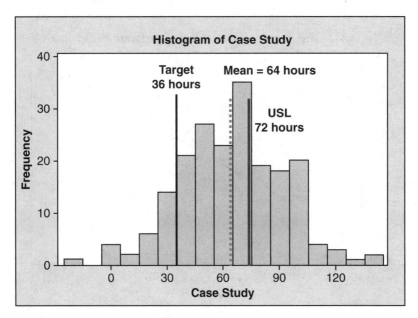

The team just moved on to Step 11, trying to identify the root causes of poor performance.

Step 11: Identify Sources of Variation

To confirm that there is a relationship between response time and lost deals, the team members conducted a correlation study and also plotted the data using a scatter plot. Using data from two quarters, they plotted the average response time for each month and the number of lost deals (see Figure 3.24). Using statistical software, the correlation coefficient r was calculated to be 0.979. Since this value is very close to 1, there is a strong statistical relationship between response time and lost deals; that is, the longer it takes to respond to the customer, the higher the chances that the borrower will choose another lender.

Figure 3.24   Case Study Scatter Plot

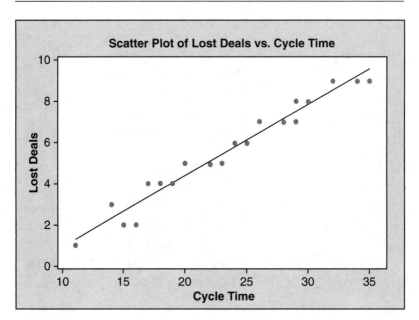

Now that the team members understood the relationship between cycle time and lost deals, they needed to determine whether the competitor was really much better at responding to customers. To find the answer, they conducted a hypothesis test. They compared their response time to that of their competitors. Using a *t* test, they set up the following test:

$$H_0: \mu_{\text{Company}} = \mu_{\text{Competitors}}$$

Null hypothesis: average cycle time for the company = average cycle time for competitors

$$H_a: \mu_{\text{Company}} \neq \mu_{\text{Competitors}}$$

Alternative hypothesis: average cycle time for the company $\neq$ average cycle time for competitors.

Using statistical software, the results of the t test are:

	Average
Cycle time—company	2.7
Cycle time—competitors	1.5

p value $= 0.0$

The company's competitors are responding to a borrower within 36 hours (1.5 days) of having received his information, whereas the company is responding after 64 hours (2.7 days). The p value of less than 0.05 confirms that there is a statistical difference between the performance of the company and its competitors (when the p value is less than 0.05, the null hypothesis is rejected). Armed with the statistical confirmation that the company is facing better-performing competitors, the team moves into the Improve phase.

C H A P T E R

IMPROVE

he Improve phase (see Figure 4.1) is focused on selecting the improvement ideas that were either identified by the team or determined through data analysis. It is also in this phase that the implementation plan is developed. There is only one step in this phase:

Step 12: Identify the Vital Xs and Implementable Solutions

If the project goal is to reduce cycle time or improve flow, tools such as 5S, line balancing, and *kaizen* are appropriate. More complex projects, where the relationships between variables are not well understood, will rely on Six Sigma tools like regression.

The key deliverables in this phase are:

- If the team is working on "quick hit" improvement opportunities, leveraging *kaizen* principles
- Introduction to additional Lean tools:
  ○ 5 S
  ○ Line balancing

Figure 4.1   Overview of Improve Phase

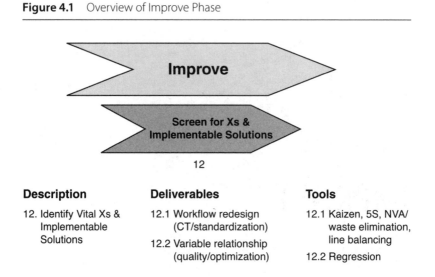

Description	Deliverables	Tools
12. Identify Vital Xs & Implementable Solutions	12.1 Workflow redesign (CT/standardization) 12.2 Variable relationship (quality/optimization)	12.1 Kaizen, 5S, NVA/ waste elimination, line balancing 12.2 Regression

- Development of a strategy for improvement
- Development of a new process or solution and working with functional managers to pilot the solution
- Establishment of team "buy-in" and the start of the handoff process to the functional manager

STEP 12: IDENTIFY THE VITAL XS AND IMPLEMENTABLE SOLUTIONS

Figure 4.2 shows the road map of tool utilization in this phase.

The tools that you select are heavily dependent on the goals and objectives of your project. However, to make certain that you are heading down the right path, you should determine whether the Xs you have identified (vital Xs) as being in need of improvement are critical elements or operating parameters. The definitions for these terms are:

Figure 4.2   Improve Phase Road Map

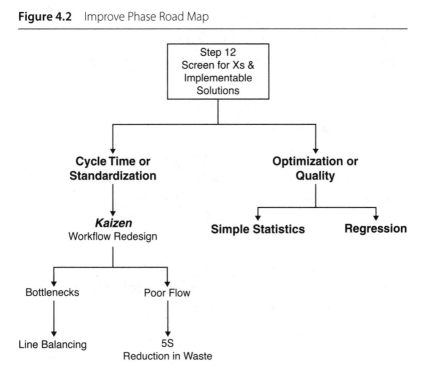

1. **Critical elements.** Xs that usually change in type rather than amount. They are not necessarily measurable on a specific scale, but they have an effect on the process. An optimal setting can be identified by testing alternatives.

   Examples are process flow and process standardization.

2. **Operating parameters.** Xs that can be changed by an amount. In order to understand their effect on a Y, multiple X levels have to be studied. An optimal setting can be identified using a mathematical model. Examples are system upload speed, recovery, process cycle time, and patient turnaround time.

Based on these definitions, if your vital Xs are critical elements, Lean tools are optimal for identifying solutions. Conversely, Six Sigma is best suited for improving Xs that fall into the category of operating parameters.

Kaizen and Lean Tools

Up until now, at each phase of the project, you may have used Lean tools to answer the required questions of that phase. A sample of tools that you may have used up to this point includes:

In the Define and Measure phases:

Map the process in detail (walk the talk!)
Product synchronization map—identifying major milestones, process options, and percent of rework.

In the Analyze phase:

Value-adding/non-value-adding analysis of process steps—identifying improvement opportunities
Determine *takt* time (available hours/customer demand)—determining the process "drumbeat," the required head count, and potential bottlenecks
- Calculate demand at capacity
- Calculate effective hours
- Create cycle time/*takt* time bar chart

This brings us to the Improve phase and the *kaizen* tool. With all the critical process information in hand (that is, how the process flows, where there is rework or fallout, non-value-adding activities, the required drumbeat for the business, and head count at each process step), we can use *kaizen* to drive to the right solution set.

What Is *Kaizen*?

Kaizen literally means change for the better. The word comes from the Japanese characters *kai*, "to take apart," and *zen*, "to make good." It is a process quality tool in which instances of waste are eliminated one by one, at minimal cost, by workers pooling their ideas and increasing efficiency in a timely manner. And most important, its philosophy is based on continuous improvement—*you cannot get to the ideal solution in one step.*

What Defines a Successful *Kaizen* Event?

Kaizen is focused on improving process flow and efficiency by eliminating waste. Ultimately, we are ensuring that the implemented improvements are sustained. The main objectives of a *kaizen* event are to:

- Enhance capacity
- Reduce non-value-adding activities or waste
- Increase productivity
- Reduce inventory
- Improve layout or flow

A quick way to assess whether any of the stated objectives have been successfully met is to ask the following questions at the end of the event:

1. **Sort.** Has the workflow been *arranged* and *prioritized?* For example, are the oldest deals in the backlog being reviewed first?
2. **Simplify.** Have we *prevented* problems from occurring? For example, have we ensured that all required data are available before work is passed to the next step?
3. **Sweep.** Has the work area been *cleaned up*? For example, are overdue or missing items identified quickly?

4. **Standardize.** Have we *defined tasks* clearly? For example, is there a uniform understanding of what is a "clean" file that is ready to send to Audit?

5. **Sustain.** How have we ensured that the *new habits developed will stay in place*? For example, what incentives or measurements can we put in place to ensure a shift in employee behavior?

In the end, *kaizen* events should:

Reduce	Increase
Cost	Productivity
Defects	Customer satisfaction
Lead time	Profit
Inventory	Customer responsiveness capacity

What Is Considered Waste?

Waste is any activity that doesn't add value to the end product or service. To better identify waste, you can ask two questions about any process step or service:

1. Is the customer willing to pay for this activity?
2. Does this activity affect the form, fit, or function of the product or service?

If you answer no to either of these questions, then you have identified waste, otherwise known as non-value-adding activity.

Examples of waste that need to be identified and eliminated include:

Signatures	Inventory (work pending review or approval)
Approvals	Overtime

Waiting   Multiple handoffs

Rework   Customer complaints or external "failures"

Just remember that from a Lean perspective, only 1 to 10 percent of activities are truly value-adding. The rest fall into the non-value-adding or necessary non-value-adding (for example, regulatory or compliance requirements) categories.

Kaizen Event Roles and Responsibilities

In every *kaizen* event, there are different parties involved at the various stages, each with specific roles and responsibilities. Knowing about these specific roles and their main objectives is necessary if the event is to be successful. The key players and their responsibilities are:

- **Quality champion or Master Black Belt.** This person sets the agenda and strategic direction, provides focus, assigns resources, and defines accountability for driving culture change. MBBs help choose the initial topic(s) for the *kaizen* event.
- *Kaizen* **sponsor or functional manager.** This person is accountable for success of the specific *kaizen* event. He removes barriers and drives implementation of results.
- **Change agent.** Also known as the *kaizen* facilitator, she is an expert in the application of change management and *kaizen* methodology. She partners with the sponsor to prepare and design the session. Ultimately, she is responsible for leading and facilitating the session.
- *Kaizen* **participants.** The participants provide content expertise to solve the problem or issue. They are the owners of the suggested improvements and ensure that the recommendations and action plans are implemented.

Typical *Kaizen* Event

Every *kaizen* event, regardless of its duration, will go through roughly the same set of milestones, starting with "event kick-off" and ending with "report out and decision action plan." Figure 4.3 provides an outline of the various stages of an event.

Figure 4.3   *Kaizen* Meeting

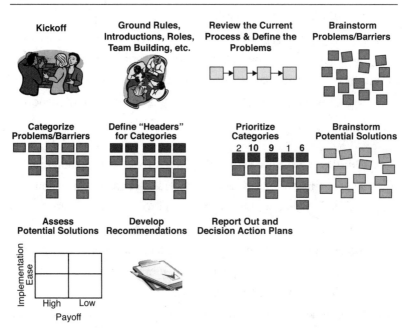

In every *kaizen* event, the team has to be introduced to the problem and the goal. The business case developed in the Define phase can help serve this purpose. The process map and the process and/or customer data collected along the way should be presented and discussed with the team members. This allows everyone to better understand the need for improvement and the potential list of issues. Through brainstorming, the problems on the list can be solidi-fied, categorized, and prioritized. The team is also responsible for identifying possible solutions. However, before presenting the list of solutions, the team should prioritize these solutions based on an ease of implementation vs. benefit analysis. The final report will then be presented to the *kaizen* champion and key stakeholders, who, in turn, have to approve the list of recommendations. It is then the responsibility of the change agent and the participants to develop an action plan, with specific "to-dos" for each participant and due dates assigned. All improvements should be implemented within 90 days, and the *kaizen* is then closed out.

Eight Rules of *Kaizen*

In order to keep the team focused on delivering meaningful results and to avoid getting stuck on discussions of how "we tried this before" and "this will never work," the following rules for *kaizen* events may prove to be helpful:

1. Discard conventional fixed ideas concerning processes.
2. Think of how to do something, not why it cannot be done.
3. Do not accept excuses. Start by observing and questioning current practices.
4. Correct mistakes at once.
5. Ask "why" five times and seek root causes.
6. Seek the wisdom of ten people rather than the knowledge of one person.
7. Do not seek perfection. Do something right away, even if only for 50 percent of the target.
8. Have fun!

Additional Lean Tools and Principles

Additional concepts that you can use in a *kaizen* event (a Lean concept itself) to help facilitate the identification of solutions are 5S and line balancing.

5S

During an eight-hour day, how much of the time is actually spent working rather than being wasted in searching for information or files, or walking to retrieve faxes or printouts? How much of your time is wasted on correcting mistakes because you are using inaccurate or outdated information? The 5S principles help to identify and address these issues.

The term 5S refers to five Japanese words that start with the letter *S*. They are the foundation blocks upon which we help create a Lean process with visual control and standard operations. The five words are:

Seiton	Tidiness
Seiri	Organization
Seiso	Cleanliness
Seiketsu	Purity
Shitsuke	Discipline

Here is a further discussion of these words.

1. ***Seiton.*** Sort through the items in the area and sort them out. Distinguish between needed and unneeded items in the area. Remove what is not needed, such as equipment, documents, desks, file cabinets, and work in progress (WIP) in queues or supplies.
2. ***Seiri.*** Organize the necessary items close to where they are needed and in such a way that any waste or abnormality is

apparent. Create locations that are self-explanatory, provide simple labeling, and set limits for quantities.

3. *Seiso.* Cleaning is a form of inspection. Ensure that documents, files, and the entire workplace shines.

4. *Seiketsu.* Standardizing is about creating guidelines for keeping the area organized and orderly. This principle can also apply to how we design processes so that everyone follows the same set of rules, steps, and principles, mitigating potential risk.

5. *Shitsuke.* This principle is about creating the right discipline and scrupulously sticking to the rules. The required level of discipline is achieved when the proper habits are formed.

At first glance, 5S may seem to be nothing but an office-cleaning exercise, but in reality, these are principles to be followed in designing new processes and workplace layouts. The 5S principles can help reduce non-value-adding activity by as much as 25 percent. That is time that can be allocated to revenue-generating activities.

Line Balancing

Line balancing and *takt* time are related concepts. Line balancing involves *distributing the work content* of the various operations in a process in such a way that the time required for each operation is equal to or less than the *takt* time of the line. Line balancing is used to:

1. Avoid a buildup of work in progress.
2. Begin identifying the number of resources required to run the "line."

This ensures the optimal usage of personnel, while meeting customer demand. Figure 4.4 outlines the benefits of line balancing.

Figure 4.4   Line Balancing

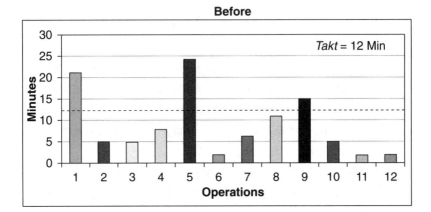

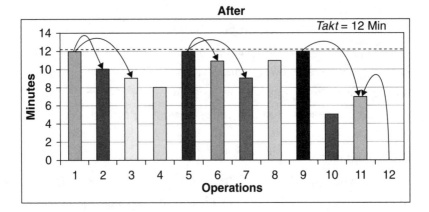

As outlined in Figure 4.4, there are 12 distinct steps in the process. The calculated *takt* time required to meet customer demand is 12 minutes. This means that every step has to complete its required task within 12 minutes. While some steps can complete their tasks in far less than 12 minutes (which can be translated as having excess capacity), others, like Step 5, exceed that requirement. Any process step that exceeds *takt* time will act as a bottleneck. The graphic demonstrates that through consolidation of process steps and reallocation of work, resources can be better utilized, there are fewer steps, and each step is capable of meeting *takt* time.

There are four distinct strategies for overcoming line-balancing challenges:

1. Reduce non-value-adding activities in process steps where the cycle time exceeds *takt* time.
2. Relocate the work, grouping tasks into segments of work equal to or less than *takt* time.
3. Use overtime.
4. Add resources or additional equipment.

Figure 4.5 shows how the elimination of non-value-adding activities helps bring balance back to the process.

Elimination or Reduction of Non-Value-Adding Activities

As discussed in the *takt* time and 5S sections, one of the main goals of a *kaizen* event is to improve capacity and process capability by eliminating non-value-adding activities. The upcoming example is from a brokerage firm, where a team is focused on improving the performance of the wire transfer process. A common process in most financial institutions, this is a very time-sensitive activity that involves great risk for both the institution and the client who is requesting the transfer (wrong amount, wrong recipient, or unavailable funds). Once the team developed a process map of the "as-is" state, it leveraged the *kaizen* event to gain consensus on which activities were non-value-adding activities, prioritize them, and reengineer the process. Figures 4.6 and 4.7 show the before and after picture.

Figure 4.5   Process Improvement

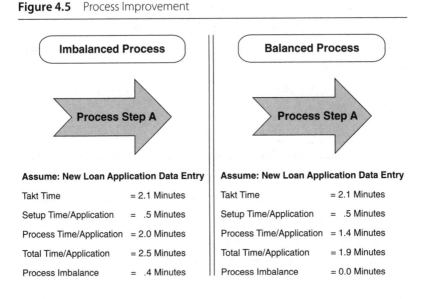

Imbalanced Process	**Balanced Process**
Process Step A	Process Step A
Assume: New Loan Application Data Entry	**Assume: New Loan Application Data Entry**
Takt Time	= 2.1 Minutes	Takt Time	= 2.1 Minutes
Setup Time/Application	= .5 Minutes	Setup Time/Application	= .5 Minutes
Process Time/Application	= 2.0 Minutes	Process Time/Application	= 1.4 Minutes
Total Time/Application	= 2.5 Minutes	Total Time/Application	= 1.9 Minutes
Process Imbalance	= .4 Minutes	Process Imbalance	= 0.0 Minutes

Figure 4.6   Process Before *Kaizen*

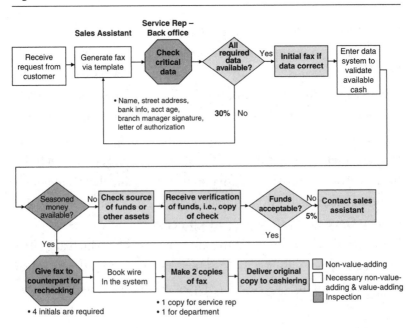

Figure 4.7 Process After *Kaizen*

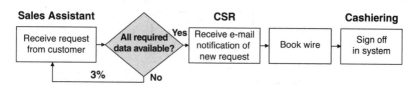

The results after a two-day event were:

- Reduced the number of steps from 14 to 5
- Eliminated four inspection points
- Reduced the process rejection and rework by 85 percent
- Reduced the overall process cycle time by over 70 percent

Kaizen Summary

You can use a *kaizen* event to identify and implement solutions involving cycle time and standardization efforts. Here are some principles for this process:

- Ensure that all bottlenecks, inefficiencies, and waste have been identified prior to engaging in *kaizen*.
- Create a cross-functional team—all members who are affected by the process should be involved.
- Remove bottlenecks using line balancing:
  - Balance tasks by *takt* time.
  - Reduce transit time.
  - Reduce manual work time.
  - Improve workflow by using 5S and reducing waste.

Six Sigma Tools

Not all project goals can be met by using Lean principles. What if you are considering changing service providers or vendors? How will you

Figure 4.8   Lean and Six Sigma Tools

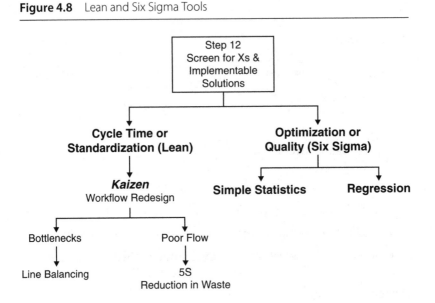

know if the new vendor's performance is statistically better? What if you have found multiple factors that affect your process—how will you know which ones have the most statistical significance? The answers to these questions can be attained by using Six Sigma tools, namely hypothesis testing (discussed in Chapter 3, "Analyze") and regression (see Figure 4.8).

Simpler Statistics—Going Back to What We Know

While there are many statistical tools for the analysis and graphical display of data, the objective of Six Sigma is to use whatever is appropriate to get the required answers. And this means that sometimes there are simpler principles that can yield the required findings. The objective of all Green Belts and Black Belts is to keep it statistically simple (KISS). To demonstrate this point, a regional bank was considering switching its checkbook issuance vendor. Based on historical performance, it knew that the time of year and the type of checkbook the client requested affected the delivery cycle time. It asked the new vendor under consideration (Vendor B) to provide information on its delivery cycle time for a period of two years. Using hypothesis testing, the bank could then determine whether its existing vendor (Vendor A) was performing better than or the same as the new vendor under consideration. Here is how the bank set up the test: for the null hypothesis, it assumed that the average delivery cycle time was the same for both vendors, and for the alternative hypothesis, it assumed that the cycle times of the two vendors were different.

$$H_0: \mu_A = \mu_B$$
$$H_a: \mu_A \neq \mu_B$$

Figure 4.9 shows the Minitab box plot and statistical analysis output from hypothesis testing.

Figure 4.9   Box Plot for Hypothesis Testing

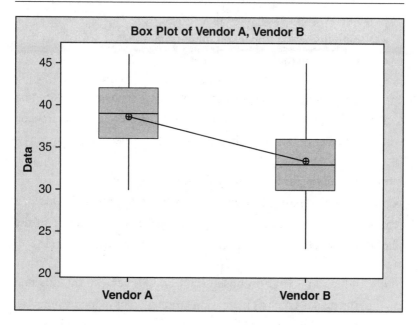

	N	Mean
Vendor A	20,500	38
Vendor B	25,040	33

p value $= 0.000$

Each vendor has provided more than 20,000 data points (denoted by the column labeled N), and the average delivery time for Vendor A is 38 days compared with 33 days for Vendor B. Since we have a p value less than 0.05, we can conclude that we need to reject the null hypothesis. Therefore, there is a statistical difference between Vendor A and Vendor B. Based on the box plot, Vendor B does perform better.

The next step for the bank is to consider the following items before making the switch and piloting the new vendor:

- Is the vendor qualified?
- Are there practical issues (location, other CTQs)?
- Is one vendor easier to work with?
- What will be the impact on other processes?
- What will be the impact on cost?

The use of hypothesis testing, a common yet powerful Six Sigma tool, provided the team with critical information on whether to proceed with the project or abandon the idea of making the switch.

Introduction to the Idea of Piloting Solutions

A pilot involves testing a process improvement on a small scale in a real business environment, whenever feasible. The objective of the pilot is to collect and analyze real process data in order to:

- Confirm that your proposed solution will achieve the targeted performance (such as increasing production or reducing defects).
- Identify any potential implementation problems (technology, training, and so on) prior to full-scale implementation.

If piloting the improvement is an option, then the team needs to define what a realistic environment looks like. The team needs to ensure that the conditions of the pilot reflect the true business conditions. That is, the new improvement should really experience all the possible process variations (region, shift, request type, or product type). A sample list of questions to consider when setting up a pilot is:

1. Should the pilot be conducted in one region or many? If many, should the pilots in the different regions be done simultaneously or one by one?
2. How long should the pilot go on?
3. Should weekends, holidays, and/or peak periods be included?
4. Who should participate? Should it be the best, worst, or average workers?
5. Which product types should be included?
6. How will the process data be collected?

If a pilot is done correctly, the benefits that will be attained include:

- Better understanding of the effects of your solution on the organization and the customer
- Proper planning for a successful full-scale implementation
- The ability to release an early version of your solution to a particular market segment that has an urgent need for the change
- Lowering your risk of failing to meet your improvement goals when the solution is fully implemented
- More accurate prediction of the monetary savings resulting from your solution
- Justification of the investment required for full-scale implementation
- Identification of potential problems with the solution implementation on a larger scale

Linear Regression

Do missing data points on an application affect loan processing cycle time? Is there a relationship between the number of patients that need to be admitted to the ward and wait time? We can use graphical tools like a scatter plot to demonstrate a relationship pictorially, but is the relationship statistically significant? Figure 4.10 is a scatter plot of the number of missing data points on a new loan application and the cycle time required to complete the "documentation" step (in which all the required customer data are compiled and the application is considered ready for underwriting) in loan processing.

Figure 4.10 Scatter Plot of Missing Data vs. Cycle Time

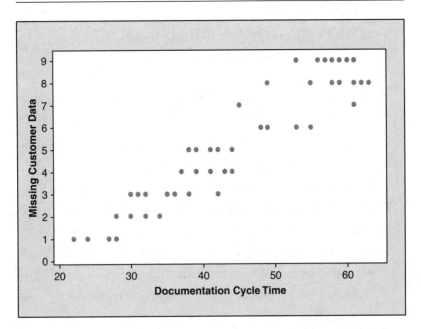

There seems to be a positive relationship between missing customer data and documentation cycle time; that is, as the number of missing data points on an application increases, so does the processing cycle time in the back office.

Regression analysis helps you further explore this relationship by building a mathematical equation that links the process Xs (for example, missing customer data) to the process output Y (for example, loan application processing cycle time). Regression is a statistical technique that is used to model and investigate the relationship between two or more variables. The model is often used for prediction: if there are three missing data points on an application, what is the expected cycle time to complete the documentation? This type of analysis begins with the team first selecting the process output, or Y, that it wants to predict—is it process cycle time, lost deals, or calls abandoned? Then the team needs to agree on a list of independent variables, or Xs, that it wants to use as predictors—for example, number of agents, applications, and missing data points. The fishbone tool and the FMEA are perfect tools for generating a list of potential Xs.

Using the same data, a regression plot can be generated using statistical software. The regression plot in Figure 4.11 has two key outputs:

- A mathematical equation linking documentation cycle time (our process output, Y) to missing data points (process input, X)
- R^2 value

The closer the R^2 value is to 100 percent, the better the prediction capability of the equation. In statistical terms, it is the fraction of the variation in the output variable that is explained by the equation. So in this case, 89 percent of the variation that we see in the documentation cycle time can be attributed to missing data in the application; the other 11 percent is affected by other variables—errors in data collection,

Figure 4.11   Regression Plot

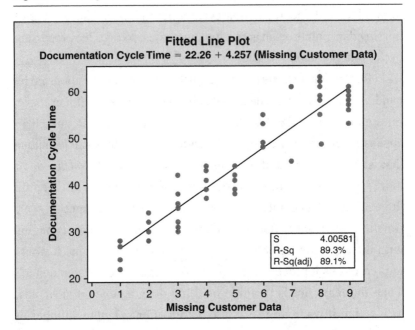

volume of applications on the days when the data were collected, the field rep filling out the application, and so on.

So how do we use this equation? Assume that we have a documentation cycle time target of 40 minutes. We can now determine the maximum number of missing data points that an application can have and still meet the cycle time requirements.

$$40 \text{ min} = 22.26 + 4.25(\text{missing data points})$$
$$4 = \text{missing data points}$$

Therefore, any application that is submitted with more than four missing data points has a high probability of missing the 40-minute processing cycle time.

What if there appears to be no relationship between your Y and X—that is, the R^2 value is very low?

That would mean that, practically speaking, the X does not influence or change your Y. More process data may not necessarily result in a relationship. Some things to consider before you abandon your data are:

- Review your data with a process expert to make sure that they make sense.
- Review your process map in conjunction with your data collection plan. Are your data hiding multiple processes, such as collecting data from multiple teams, products, or regions? When the data were being collected, combining these effects may not have seemed critical, but perhaps the lack of correlation between X and Y indicates that these effects do heavily influence the process output. As an example, if the teams work differently, or if products are sold via different channels, the outputs may be different (for example, process cycle time between teams or channels will be different), and that can affect the results of your regression. In cases where the data may reflect multiple processes, each of these processes needs to be examined individually.

IMPROVE PHASE SUMMARY

At the start of the Improve phase, the team has a good list of Xs and/or process steps that are in need of improvement. Depending on the project goals and the complexity of the required solutions, the team will have to choose between the Lean and Six Sigma tool kits. *Kaizen* events, in combination with 5S; VA, NVA, NNVA; and line-balancing principles, are reserved for improving process flow and speed, whereas regression and simpler statistical tools discussed in the Analyze phase (hypothesis testing) are used to ensure that we are fixing the appropriate Xs by the right amount. Either path should yield significant improvements that can be measured and quantified. Moving to the next phase, Control, is an indication that appropriate gains have been attained, and that the team's focus is now centered on ensuring the sustainability of those gains.

IMPROVE PHASE CHECKLIST

☑ Define a short list of Xs.

☑ Ensure that all your Xs are really controllable and that you don't have any Ys in the list.

☑ Establish your improvement approach—regression, simple statistics, or *kaizen*.

☑ If you are pursuing a *kaizen* event, you have the necessary support to implement the suggested improvements.

☑ The R^2 value attained in regression has an acceptable level of predictability.

☑ Have a final and short list of vital Xs.

QUESTIONS TO ASK AT THE END OF THE IMPROVE PHASE

1. What vital Xs have you uncovered?

2. Were you able to resolve your process challenges with a *kaizen* event? Will more such events be needed?

3. How sure are you of your results? Did anything surprise you?

APPLICATION OF LEAN SIX SIGMA CASE STUDY— IMPROVE PHASE DELIVERABLES

The continuation of the case study illustrates the Improve phase of a Lean Six Sigma project.

Step 12: Identify the Vital Xs and Implementable Solutions

In the Measure phase, using a fishbone, the team agreed that the manual data entry process had the largest impact on the overall process cycle time. In the Improve phase, the team had to understand why. Using the same tool, the fishbone, the team conducted another brainstorming session, and the results pointed to one central reason: missing critical information. As outlined in the fishbone diagram in Figure 4.12, some of the main reasons for missing critical customer information were:

1. The method by which information was received (mail, e-mail, or fax)
2. Whether a list of required documents was provided to the customer (borrower)
3. The varying types of documentation requested by the operations team from the borrower

Figure 4.12   Case Study Fishbone Diagram

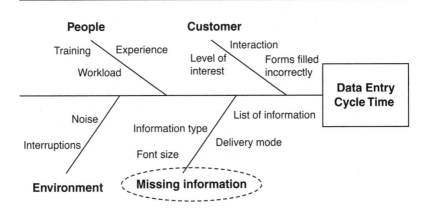

To validate this theory, the team used regression to determine the mathematical relationship between missing information and process cycle time. And sure enough, with a high adjusted R^2 value of close to 90 percent, there is a strong relationship between missing data and cycle time. The regression equation is:

Documentation cycle time $= 22.26 + 4.257$(missing customer data)

Therefore, if the team needs to target the process at 36 hours in order to meet the customer-expected response time of 72 hours, the maximum number of missing data that any file can have is:

$$36 = 22.26 + 4.257\text{(missing data)}$$
$$\text{Missing data} = 3.2 \text{ data points}$$

Now the team has to determine what elements in the process of customer data collection it needs to change in order to never exceed three missing data points. To find the right answer, it has to set up an experiment, a process known as design of experiment (DOE). This topic was not covered in the book, as it requires advanced statistical knowledge. If you think that modifying multiple process parameters will be required to find the right answer, then you will need the advice and help of a statistician. For this case study, the team knew that the critical drivers of missing data were:

1. The method by which information was received (e-mail vs. mail)
2. Whether or not a list of required items was provided to the borrower
3. Whether the company had asked for one or two years of financial data

The team set up an experiment in which one, two, or all three variables were changed and the documentation cycle time was measured. The objective was to test the process under all possible conditions. The results of the experiment were studied using statistical software. The team concluded that the process cycle time was significantly reduced when a list of required items was provided to the borrower and she was asked to e-mail all information. Asking for one vs. two years of financial information had minimal impact on overall cycle time.

The team must now pilot these solutions to confirm the results of the experiment and develop control plans for long-term sustainability.

CONTROL

The last phase of Lean Six Sigma is Control (see Figure 5.1). This phase focuses on successfully passing the project to a functional owner and ensuring long-term sustainability of the improvements. There are three steps in the Control phase:

Step 13: Validate measurement system analysis on the Xs.
Step 14: Determine the process capability.
Step 15: Implement process control.

The main deliverables in this phase are:

- Assurance that the measurement system is adequate to detect differences in the performance of critical Xs
- Determination of whether project goals have been attained

- Development and implementation of control plans, ensuring that the process stays in control
- Introduction of the different types of control charts
- Knowledge of when to close out your project

Figure 5.1   Overview of Control Phase

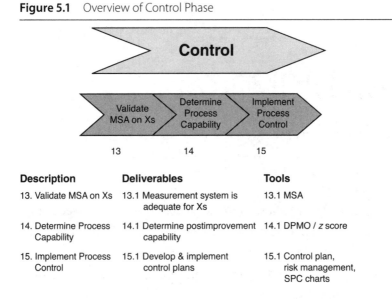

Description	Deliverables	Tools
13. Validate MSA on Xs	13.1 Measurement system is adequate for Xs	13.1 MSA
14. Determine Process Capability	14.1 Determine postimprovement capability	14.1 DPMO / z score
15. Implement Process Control	15.1 Develop & implement control plans	15.1 Control plan, risk management, SPC charts

STEP 13: VALIDATE MEASUREMENT SYSTEM ANALYSIS ON THE XS

To arrive at the deliverables in Steps 13 and 14, we can rely on tools that were discussed in the Measure and Analyze phases. Step 13 is about ensuring that we have an adequate and reliable way of measuring the critical Xs of the process. In the Improve phase, we discovered the critical elements that affect our process performance, that is, critical Xs. We also discovered the critical limits for each X if we wanted the process to perform in a specific way—for example, to get a loan approved within five days, we need the complete set of borrower's information by the second day; anything beyond that will would cause us to miss our five-day commitment. Or to keep patient wait time at 15 minutes, we need at least two triage nurses available at all times. And so the team needs to determine how to:

1. Actively track and measure these numbers
2. Ensure that the method by which Xs are been measured is reliable and accurate

This brings us back to the measurement system analysis discussed in the Measure phase. The team can leverage the same principles used to ensure that the measurement system was valid for the process output (Y) and ensure that the system is also adequate for X.

STEP 14: DETERMINE THE PROCESS CAPABILITY

As for Step 14, before we implement the control plans, we first need to ensure that we have actually achieved our goals. To do this, we need to statistically confirm our improvements:

1. Calculate the post improvement performance capability, using the technique described in Step 9.
2. Confirm that the improvement goal established in Step 2 has affected the Y.
3. If it has not, go back to Step 11 to look for additional sources of variation.

STEP 15: IMPLEMENT PROCESS CONTROL

When we have completed Steps 13 and 14, we can start to develop the required control plans.

What Is a Process Control System?

A process control system is a strategy for maintaining the improved process performance over time. It outlines the specific actions and tools required for sustaining process improvements or gains. There are several ways to develop a control system:

- Risk management
- *Poka-yoke*—mistake-proofing devices
- Statistical process control (SPC)
- Data collection plans
- Ongoing measurements
- Audit plans
- Process documentation
- Process ownership

A process control system is critical for all projects because it helps to:

- Define the actions, resources, and responsibilities required to make sure that the problem remains corrected and that the benefits from the solution continue to be realized.
- Provide the methods and tools needed to maintain the process improvement, *independent of the current team.*
- Ensure that the improvements made have been documented (this is often necessary to meet regulatory requirements).

- Ease full-scale implementation by promoting a common understanding of the process and planned improvements.

While there are several ways to develop a process control system, we will discuss the three most common methods (see Figure 5.2).

Figure 5.2   Three Categories of Control Mechanisms

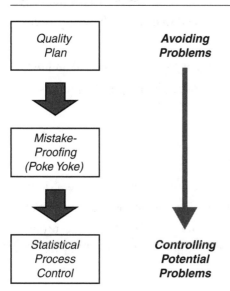

What Is a Quality Plan?

A *quality plan* is a *documented plan* whose purpose is to *ensure* that each product or service characteristic or process requirement stays in *conformance*. Examples of these documented plans include the final state process map, checklists, or the newly documented standard operating procedures. Ideally, a quality plan should include:

1. Process standards, such as procedures to follow, specifications, or operating tolerances.

2. A description of the process flow and documentation of roles and responsibilities—a flowchart is very useful.

3. A description of the new standard operating procedures (SOPs). SOPs have to be very specific, telling the employees precisely what actions to take and when and where to take them. The descriptions need to be at a level such that the job can be performed well by a person who is not fully trained. And finally, they need to describe how to prevent process variation.

4. Process controls, that is, items to be monitored or audited, and the corresponding response planning if the process should deviate.

What Is Mistake-Proofing?

Mistake-proofing, also known as the Lean tool *poka-yoke*, is a technique for eliminating errors by making it impossible for mistakes to occur. When you are applying the concept of mistake-proofing in developing a control plan, it is important to remember its guiding principles:

- *Respect* the intelligence of employees (mistakes are the fault of processes, not people).
- Eliminate high-volume *repetitive* tasks or actions that require employees to constantly be alert.
- *Free* employees' time and mind to pursue more creative and value-adding activities.
- It is *not acceptable* to produce even a small number of defects or defective products.
- The objective is *zero defects.*

If we understand the root cause of errors, we can better define solutions. Generally the main drivers of errors are:

- Incorrect procedures or operational definitions
- Excessive variation in the process or its inputs
- Inaccurate measuring devices
- Human error

Examples of things in our everyday lives that have been mistake-proofed include:

- Irons that shut off automatically
- ATM stations that accept debit cards only if they are inserted correctly
- Cars that stop automatically if a seatbelt is not worn

How Is Mistake-Proofing Different from Traditional Inspection Processes?

Many organizations have dedicated people or use portions of people's time to review other employees' work or to audit the end product or service for quality control on a regular basis. In these organizations, errors are caught after human labor and cost have been applied to develop and deliver the product or service. More important, this mode of inspection relies on humans to catch errors, and this is not 100 percent effective. The key reason why firms rely on inspection instead of mistake-proofing has to do with the traditional view of errors rather than the Lean Six Sigma view of errors.

- The traditional view of errors is that they are inevitable, because:
  - People are only human.
  - There is variation in everything.

- o Lack of standard operating procedures results in each person having his own way of doing things.
- o Inspection is necessary.
- The Lean Six Sigma view on errors is that they can be eliminated.
  - o Not all errors can be eliminated, but many can, and others can be reduced.
  - o The more errors we can eliminate, the better our quality.
  - o The need for inspection can be reduced or eliminated.

Figure 5.3 helps to outline the difference between traditional quality control plans that rely on inspection and a mistake-proofed process.

Figure 5.3   Feedback

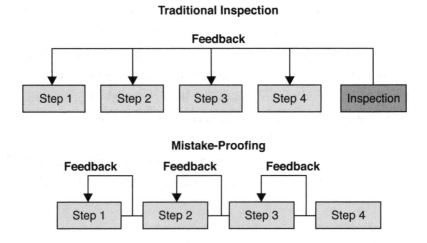

The key differences between traditional inspection and mistake-proofing are given in Table 5.1.

Table 5.1   Key Differences Between Traditional Inspection and Mistake-Proofing

Traditional Inspection	Mistake-Proofing
Defects are occurring at every possible step in the process, with compounding effects.	Every unit is inspected in a 100 percent informative inspection—workers know what to look for and what defines quality in a work product.
Errors and defects are caught at the end of the process.	Immediate feedback on errors and defects is required so that action can be taken.
Does not allow for an effective feedback loop of information with upstream process steps.	Relies on both self and successive checking of work quality.
Causes much wasted effort—labor, cost, material, and so on.	Helps to avoid producing additional units with the same defect.

In the end, you cannot inspect quality into a process; you have to build it in.

Steps in Mistake-Proofing

The steps required for mistake-proofing are rather simple, but they do rely on the expertise of the process, product, or service subject-matter experts. The steps are shown in Figure 5.4.

The advantages of mistake-proofing are that:

- No formal training is required to get the team started.
- It can help to eliminate many inspection points.
- It relieves employees from repetitive tasks, which helps them focus on value-adding activities.
- It results in defect-free work.
- It provides immediate action when problems arise.

Figure 5.4 *Poka-yoke*

1. *Identify* where errors occur	2. *Prioritize* the problems
• Brainstorming	• Frequency vs. impact
• Customer complaints	• Wasted labor
• Defective service/part analyses	• Rework time/detection time
• Error reports	• Detection cost/overall cost
• Failure modes and effects analysis (FMEA)	• Lost customers
3. Seek out the *root cause*	**4. Create *solutions***
• Do not cover up problems or treat symptoms	• Make it impossible to do it wrong
• Correct errors at their source	• Cost/benefit analysis
• Other methods to determine the root cause are:	– How long will it take for the solution to pay for itself?
– Ask "why" five times	• Think outside of the box
– Fishbone diagrams	
– Brainstorming	
– Stratification	

When you are applying the mistake-proofing principle with your team, just remember:

- Your goal is to build quality into your process(es).
- All inadvertent errors and defects can be eliminated or reduced significantly if everyone works together to identify the true causes of these errors and defects.
- Employees can stop doing things wrong and start doing them right.
- Avoid getting caught up in excuses; the team needs to think about how work can be performed error-free.

- You may not be able to eliminate an error completely, but even a 70 percent chance of success is good enough—this is all about continuous improvement.
- Seek out the *true* cause of an error, using fishbone, brainstorming, five whys, FMEA, and other tools.

Statistical Process Control

The third technique for developing a process control system is statistical process control (SPC).

What Is an SPC Chart?

An SPC chart is nothing more than a time-ordered plot of your process data (see Figure 5.5). When these data are graphed using statistical software, the resulting plot outlines the expected range of variation of the data. Since the expected range is known, anything outside of that is considered a special occurrence that needs investigation and correction.

Figure 5.5 SPC Chart

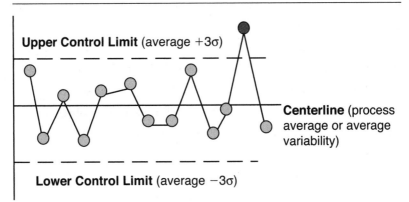

What Is the Purpose of an SPC Chart?

SPC charts can be used to monitor either your process Xs or your process Y (inputs or output), or both. When process data are readily available, these charts can help the process owner quickly identify:

- When a process is working the way it is intended to—experiencing variation, but nothing unusual or unexpected
- When the process has changed and action needs to be taken

Ultimately, SPC charts can help reduce rejects and rework, improving productivity.

Types of SPC Charts

In general, there are two categories of SPC charts: variable and attribute. Variable charts require continuous data (length, dimension, cycle time, and other such measures), and attribute charts use discrete data (good/bad, pass/fail, and other such measures). There are four types of attribute charts: NP, P, C, and U. For variable charts, there are two types: individuals and moving range, and X-bar and range.

So how does one know which chart in each category to use? The answer will depend on several variables: whether you have lots of data or a little, and whether the data set is consistent in size or variable. These factors affect the type of graph you should use. The flow chart in Figure 5.6 helps outline the selection process.

Based on your process data, you can determine what chart can be generated. Once you have collected the data, you can use statistical software to produce the appropriate chart(s) and provide

Figure 5.6   Which SPC Chart to Use

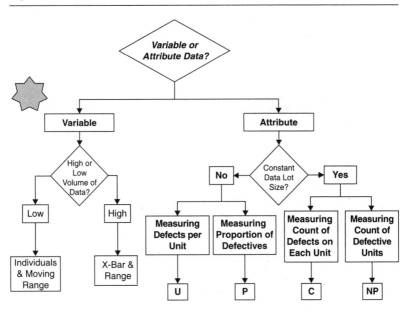

continuous monitoring of the process. Table 5.2 and Figure 5.7 provide an example of an SPC C chart for a process that is monitoring the number of missing data in incoming applications. Each application has 20 critical customer data. For 20 days, 25 random applications are collected and the total number of missing data points is monitored. A chart of the data is then produced (see Figure 5.7).

How Do You Read an SPC Chart?

When you develop an SPC chart for process Xs and/or Ys, you are monitoring the process for two types of variation:

- **Common-cause variation.** Natural and random variations, such as natural volatility in the incoming volume of requests or processing time.

- **Special-cause variation.** Unusual, unexpected, or sporadic variation, such as that caused by a financial market meltdown or equipment failure.

Table 5.2 Data Table for SPC Chart

Day	Count of Missing Data
1	10
2	8
3	7
4	6
5	15
6	17
7	4
8	8
9	6
10	16
11	3
12	11
13	9
14	10
15	11
16	7
17	5
18	3
19	10
20	4

If a process is experiencing only common-cause variation, meaning that it is in control and stable, but is not meeting customer expectations, then fundamental process changes have to be implemented. If, on the other hand, the process is experiencing special-cause variation, it is out of control and unstable, and the root cause has to be investigated immediately. Quick action has to be taken in order to avoid recurrence.

Figure 5.7   SPC Chart Example

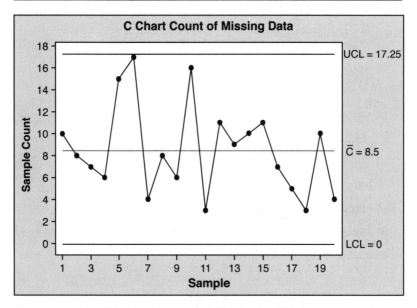

CONTROL PHASE SUMMARY

Once the improvements have been implemented, the team needs to ensure that the project goals have been attained and that the required measures for sustainability are in place. Lean principles, such as mistake-proofing, encourage the team to design the process in a way that doesn't permit errors to take place, while SPC charting allows the process outputs and inputs to be monitored. The availability of process data, the cost of collecting them, and the possibility of actually mistake-proofing a step are all key considerations in determining what type of control plan to use. Regardless of the method, the common theme among all Control phase tools remains the same: the functional owners of the improved process need to have bought into the new way of doing business. The buy-in is the ultimate Control plan that will ensure that the improvements will stay in place long after the team has been disbanded.

CONTROL PHASE CHECKLIST

- ☑ Validate that the measurement system is adequate for measuring your critical Xs.
- ☑ Verify that the process improvements that you tested in the pilot have attained the goals.
- ☑ Hand off the process to the process owners.
- ☑ Develop and implement a strategy for control, such as risk management or mistake-proofing.

QUESTIONS TO ASK AT THE END OF THE CONTROL PHASE

1. Have you validated the measurement or just your ability to read the database?
2. How large is your measurement error (as a percentage of the allowable error)?
3. Did you meet the targets? Did you meet the prediction?
4. Did you change the value of the central tendency? If so, was this a deliberate process change? If it wasn't, why did the value change?
5. What risks have you identified that could jeopardize your control strategy?
6. What actions are still required to guarantee sustainability?

APPLICATION OF LEAN SIX SIGMA CASE STUDY— CONTROL PHASE DELIVERABLES

After the process change, the team knew that in order to meet customer expectations, it had to make sure that the operations team completed the review of each packet within 36 hours. To attain this operational goal, the incoming packet had to be received via e-mail, and no packet could have more than three critical customer data points missing from it. Prior to implementing a control plan, the team had to ensure that they had an accurate and reliable process for collecting data on the critical Xs (missing data points and receipt of info via e-mail). Since the data collection process will be 100 percent manual, they trained the future data collectors on the how to identify and record a defect. After running a repeatability and reproducibility test (discussed in Measure phase), the team was comfortable that they had a reliable data collection process.

Prior to the improvements, the team members had collected data on the number of missing data points in each packet (they used these data to determine whether there was a relationship between missing data and cycle time). To calculate the new process capability, and also to monitor the process, they implemented an SPC chart. On a daily basis, 40 random files were collected, and the number of missing data points was counted. This process was repeated for 20 days (similar to the data collection process prior to the improvements). The data were plotted using a C chart, and they indicated that the average number of missing data points for the 40 files on a daily basis was about 1.15 (see Figure 5.8). However, there was one instance in which four data points were missing. So is the process better? To answer this question, the team compared the before and after process capability for receiving customer data.

Figure 5.8 Case Study SPC Chart

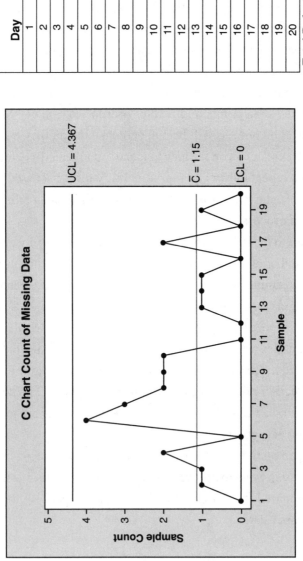

Day	Count of Missing Data
1	0
2	1
3	1
4	2
5	0
6	4
7	3
8	2
9	2
10	2
11	0
12	0
13	1
14	1
15	1
16	0
17	2
18	0
19	1
20	0
Total Defects	23

Before	After
Units = 40 × 20 days = 800	Units = 40/day × 20 days = 800
Total number of defects = 267	Total number of defects = 23
DPMO = (267/800) × 1,000,000 = 333,750	DPMO = (23/800) × 1,000,000 = 28,750
z score (using z table) = 1.9	z score (using z table) = 3.4

The team was able to gain substantial improvements in terms of the reduction in error rates and improved process capability (z score). With a good control plan for one of the process's critical Xs (missing data points), the team's final step will be to develop a control chart for the process Y: response time to the customer.

6

CONCLUSION

s a project inches closer to completion, the Green and Black Belts must start thinking about how to wrap up all the work that they have put into the project. The end of a project and the decommissioning of a project team is much like a "little death." It is common for team members to want to prolong the team's existence beyond the time when it is useful. Often such a strong bond has been forged within the team that its members find it difficult to let go.

If project completion is to go smoothly, the team leader will need to leverage various resources that are available within the organization. The leadership team should also help the team members bring the project to a graceful close. It will be critical for the leaders to recognize the different stages that people may go through. The leaders will need to establish that the project has indeed come to an end and emphasize that there are other opportunities available for the team members to focus on. This is accomplished through a sympathetic affirmation of the work the team has put into the project. It is important to establish the end of this group, even though its members will continue to have contact with one another in other venues.

The project leader may have a celebration event that officially marks the end of the project. He can provide a souvenir (coffee mug, plaque, T-shirt, or something similar) of the project team and its project, help members articulate their appreciation, and hopefully help them move on to other projects.

If this is to be accomplished, the team members must be confident of the following:

- The purpose of the project has been fulfilled.
- The original goals for improvement have been achieved and/or there has been substantial improvement in the process.
- It's clear that any further improvement will require a new major breakthrough effort (for example, new technology).
- Staff members have incorporated the discoveries of the project team into their work and are now actively involved in further improvement efforts.

To make sure we are not being hasty in wrapping up the project, all the questions in the following list generally need to be answered in the affirmative:

- Did the team achieve its goal?
- Do the data show that the new process is stable and under control?
- Do the data show that the new process is capable of meeting customer requirements?
- Has the new sigma level met or exceeded the goal?

- Do the financials show the benefit to the organization?
- Has the team documented the new process?
- Has the team documented best practices?
- Have the dashboard vital signs or ongoing metrics been implemented?
- Has the process owner received all the documentation and does she understand the monitoring process, including how to respond to changes in the metrics?

For the project to be successful in ways that really get the leadership team excited, the team needs to show that it has delivered a financial benefit. At the Improve phase of the project, the anticipated financial benefits were based on best-guess estimates and assumptions, with the help of the finance team. But as the project comes to an end, there should be more evidence of the financial impact that the new process is having. Documenting the financial benefits justifies the value of the project—it shows that there were real benefits from the effort.

PROJECT DOCUMENTATION

The team has gained a significant amount of knowledge as it has followed the path of DMAIC. This knowledge includes specific information concerning both content (discovering new information about the process, what the root cause is, and so on) and process (hypothesis testing, calculating sigma, writing CTQs, and so on). Other individuals and project teams can benefit from having access to both these types of knowledge. Sharing both this information and best practices can help shorten the subsequent learning curves for other teams.

Although you should be documenting your project as the team progresses through DMAIC, the documentation package is really finalized at the end of the project. (At this point, all uncertainty concerning any of the issues involved must be cleared up.) The following checklist will facilitate the creation of the project binder:

- Make sure that you have documented your project using the DMAIC templates.
- All data supporting your findings and analysis should be included in your project binder.
- Project documentation is the record and history of the project through the DMAIC phases.
- If additional opportunities for improvement were discovered, you should document them in the file.
- Project documentation saves and shares the steps taken, knowledge gained, lessons learned, and best practices discovered during the course of the project.

PROJECT TRANSLATION

One of the main reasons that teams are urged to create a binder that contains the critical information regarding the project is to ensure that there is no duplication of effort should another team be working on a tangentially related effort. Sharing best practices and translating findings to other parts of the organization become critical components of wrapping up the project. If there are other projects that may flow out of the original project, it behooves the team to make all data and findings available to interested parties.

LAST THOUGHTS

DMAIC is not a once-and-done journey. The quality path is one of recurrence and revisiting. An organization is never stuck in a state of perfection; it is always experiencing change and variation. Change and variation mean unhappy customers and lost revenue. For this very reason, the quality team must always be aware that there are opportunities awaiting its attention. Once a project has been completed, the team deserves to be celebrated, but this does not mean that it is time to stop looking for improvement opportunities. The most successful organizations are those that have an ingrained culture of ongoing improvement and have empowered their staff members to take bold steps in addressing their customer and organizational needs.

PROCESSARC COMPREHENSION TEST

1. In the Analyze phase, one of the things you do is:
   a. Define performance standards.
   b. Establish operating tolerances and pilot a solution.
   c. Establish process capability.
   d. Define a process map.

2. Collecting VOC helps to:
   a. Define how CTQs are linked to vital Xs.
   b. Determine how customer CTQs become project CTQs.
   c. Decide upon your improvement strategy.
   d. Design your DOE.

3. The goal statement defines:
   a. In broad terms, the measurable improvement objective.
   b. The dollar benefits of the project.

    c.   The DPMO improvement required.

    d.   The sigma score expected upon completion of the project.

4. The part of team charter development that defines and places boundaries on the process is:

    a.   The business case.

    b.   The goal statement.

    c.   Defining team roles.

    d.   Assessing the project scope.

5. The purpose of a process map is:

    a.   To create a shared view of the process and help identify key inputs.

    b.   To provide a structure for finding the causes of an effect.

    c.   To identify ways in which a subprocess or product characteristic can fail.

    d.   All of the above.

6. Components of a good performance standard include:

    a.   Target performance.

    b.   Operational definition.

    c.   Specification limits.

    d.   All of the above.

7. What is the statistic used for central tendency with normal data?

    a.   IQR (interquartile range, Q3 – Q1)

    b.   Quartile 1 (Q1)

    c.   Median

    d.   Mean

8. The importance of validating a measurement system is to ensure that the measurement does reflect the true variation of the process.

    a.   True

    b.   False

9. In the two-sample *t* test, you get a *p* value of 0.06. The results indicate that
   a. You would fail to reject the null hypothesis.
   b. You would reject the null hypothesis.

10. When you compare Process A to Process B, Process A has a *z* score of 3.6, while Process B has a *z* score of 2.8. Process B therefore is more capable in terms of meeting customer requirements.
    a. True
    b. False

11. Which of the following approaches is used to determine differences between population sets?
    a. Screening design of experiments
    b. Optimization design of experiments
    c. Hypothesis test
    d. Process capability analysis

12. *Takt* time is:
    a. The drumbeat of the process—the output required to meet demand.
    b. The frequency of incoming customer requests.
    c. The number of hours required to complete production of one piece.
    d. The amount of resources or overtime required to meet demand.

13. The purpose of a failure modes and effects analysis (FMEA) is:
    a. To provide a quantitative view used to identify a focus area.
    b. To relate the customer CTQs to measurable subprocesses or product characteristics.

   c.   To identify ways in which a subprocess or product characteristic
        can fail.
   d.   To create a shared view of the process.

14. You have a unit with five opportunities. If any opportunity is bad, the whole
    unit is bad—binomial distribution. You want to use SPC to monitor this unit.
    What control chart would you use?
    a.   The X-bar *R* chart
    b.   The U chart
    c.   The P chart
    d.   The IMR chart

15. Mistake-proofing is:
    a.   A method of identifying potential defects.
    b.   A technique for eliminating errors by making it impossible to make
         mistakes in the process.
    c.   A means of responding to defects before they leave
         the facility.
    d.   Part of statistical process control.

16. Which of the following is a measure of variation?
    a.   The upper specification limit
    b.   The standard deviation
    c.   The lower specification limit
    d.   Both (a) and (c)

17. The purpose of a *kaizen* event is to:
    a.   Define standard operations and eliminate NVA in a short period of time,
         using the expertise of everyday users.
    b.   Create a shared view of the process.
    c.   Provide a structure for finding the causes of an effect.
    d.   Provide a quantitative view used to identify a focus area.

18. In the Measure phase, one of the things you do is:
    a. Conduct a DOE.
    b. Establish process capability.
    c. Define performance standards.
    d. Define performance objectives.

19. In an FMEA, what is the RPN?
    a. The product of the severity, occurrences, and detection numbers
    b. The sum of the severity, occurrences, and detection numbers
    c. The probability of making a Type I error
    d. The probability of making a Type II error

20. If your USL is 100 days, your mean is 85 days, and your short-term standard deviation is 5 days, what is your $z_{st}(\pm 0.1)$?

21. If your z_{st} is 4, your USL is 50, and your standard deviation is 2, what is your mean?

22. The best that our process can achieve using current technology is called the:
    a. Baseline.
    b. Entitlement.
    c. Sigma value.
    d. Benchmark.

23. The null hypothesis generally presumes:
    a. No change, or the status quo.
    b. The need for immediate action.
    c. The essential leadership of the Six Sigma project team.
    d. The need for new process technology.

24. You have attribute data. Your defects are 29 out of 2,000 units with 2 quality characteristics per unit. What is your short-term z?

25. Your DPMO is 326,558. What is your short-term z value ($\pm$ 0.1)?

26. The first element of the team charter is to:
    a.   Establish the business case.
    b.   Choose the team members.
    c.   Evaluate possible improvement initiatives.
    d.   Design the DOE.

27. In defining a team, you should always define:
    a.   Roles, responsibilities, and salaries.
    b.   Roles and supervisory input.
    c.   Responsibilities and reporting structure.
    d.   Roles, responsibilities, and expectations.

28. The contents of the high-level process map include:
    a.   Customer requirements, outputs, process steps, costs, and suppliers.
    b.   Customer requirements, outputs, process steps, inputs, and suppliers.
    c.   Schedule factors, outputs, process steps, inputs, and suppliers.
    d.   None of the above.

29. The purpose of a Pareto chart is:
    a.   To identify ways in which a subprocess or product characteristic can fail.
    b.   To provide a quantitative view used to identify a focus area.
    c.   To provide a structure for finding the causes of an effect.
    d.   To create a shared view of the process.

30. You need to have an effective process control system because:
    a.   The process will have a tendency to degrade over time.
    b.   People outside of the Six Sigma team need to know how to manage the process.
    c.   Operators need to know what to do if the process gets out of control.
    d.   All of the above.

31. When validating the measurement system in the Control phase, we:
    a.   Focus on all the Xs.
    b.   Use historical data and process knowledge.
    c.   Focus on the critical Xs identified in the Improve phase.
    d.   Calculate overall measurement system repeatability, reproducibility, and accuracy.

32. In the Improve phase, one of the things you do is:
    a.   Establish a data collection plan.
    b.   Establish process capability.
    c.   Discover variable relationships.
    d.   Implement a process control system and project closure.

33. In the Control phase, one of the things you do is:
    a.   Identify CTQs.
    b.   Establish process capability.
    c.   Discover variable relationships.
    d.   Implement a process control system and project closure.

34. A variable control chart tracks:
    a.   Discrete data, such as pass/fail or good/bad.
    b.   Continuous data, such as cycle time, length, or diameter.
    c.   Several characteristics of the same process.
    d.   Responses to defects.

35. For a test with a 90-minute time limit and a minimum passing grade of 70 percent, which of these is an acceptable performance standard?
    a.   Complete the final exam within 90 minutes, with an acceptable grade.
    b.   Score at least 70 percent on the final exam.
    c.   Complete the final exam within 90 minutes, with a score of at least 70 percent correct.
    d.   Pass the final exam.

36. What is the purpose of a data collection plan?
    a. To provide a clear, documented strategy for collecting reliable data
    b. To give all team members a common reference
    c. To help to ensure that resources are used to collect only critical data
    d. All of the above

37. If your X is usually changed in type or kind, rather than amount, it is a(n):
    a. Operating parameter.
    b. DOE design.
    c. Critical element.
    d. Vital X.

38. The line in the box of a box plot represents the mean.
    a. True
    b. False

39. Overall validation of process improvement is done by:
    a. Calculating the new process capability and performing a
        hypothesis test.
    b. A process capability report.
    c. Just a hypothesis test.
    d. Generating a regression analysis on the new process.

40. Data sets A and B in Figure 7.1 show high levels of correlation.
    a. True
    b. False

Figure 7.1   Scatter Plot of Data Set A vs. Data Set B

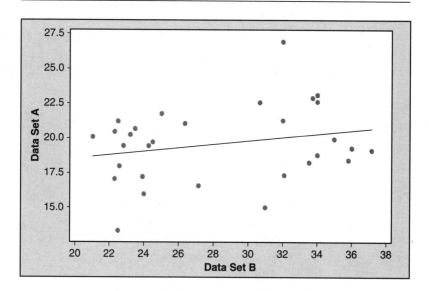

PROCESSARC COMPREHENSION TEST ANSWER KEY

1. c
2. b
3. a
4. d
5. a
6. d
7. d
8. a
9. a
10. b. The higher the z score (sigma value), the lower the probability of making an error. Therefore, Process A is more capable.

11. c
12. a
13. c
14. c
15. b
16. b
17. a
18. c
19. a
20. $z = (100 - 85)/5 = 3$
21. $4 = (50 - x)/2; x = 42$
22. b

23. a

24. Defect = 29

    Unit = 2000

    Total Opportunity = 2 × 2000 = 4000

    DPMO = (29/4000) × 1,000,000 = 7250

    Using the z/DPMO table, $z = 3.9$

25. Using a z/DPMP table, $z = 1.9$

26. a

27. d

28. b

29. b

30. d

31. c

32. c

33. d

34. b

35. c

36. d

37. c

38. b. The line represents the median.

39. a

40. b. Based on the scatter plot, there seems to be no relationship between data sets A and B. The data do not demonstrate any trends, that is, the performance level of A does not affect B.

INDEX

ABOUT THE AUTHORS

Sheila Shaffie

For more than 10 years, Sheila held leadership positions in quality and process management at three General Electric businesses: Plastics, Health Care, and Capital. As the cofounder of Process Arc, a Lean and Six Sigma training and consulting firm, a sample list of her clients includes: GMAC, Associated Bank, US Bank, Guaranty Bank, Thomson Reuters, and Allied Capital.

Sheila has a proven track record in launching global quality initiatives, managing Six Sigma process refinement, and delivering quantifiable customer satisfaction. As the director of quality, she pioneered the use of Lean and Six Sigma in GE Capital's transactional environment. Her efforts led to an 80 percent improvement in customer service levels. Sheila honed her Six Sigma, Transactional Lean, Change Management, and kaizen skills by closing out more than 250 Six Sigma projects and delivering $90 million in cost reduction. In her career at GE, she trained and led more than 100 Six Sigma Green Belts and Black Belts globally.

Sheila holds an MBA from the University of Chicago and a BS in chemical engineering from the University of Waterloo. She is GE Six Sigma Green Belt, Black Belt, and Master Black Belt certified. She has received additional training in GE's technical leadership and management development programs, as well as its change acceleration process (CAP) and CAP facilitation.

Shahbaz Shahbazi

Prior to launching ProcessArc, Shahbaz was a leader in General Electric's Global Six Sigma Quality organization focused on strategic business growth. As an expatriate based in Paris, France, he reformulated a sales and pricing strategy for a $250 million market and streamlined the commercial launch of new products. He has also led global customer satisfaction initiatives. As the cofounder of ProcessArc, he has helped institutions like RW Baird, BETA systems, Industrial Bank, Wauwatosa Savings Bank, and Metavante launch Lean Six Sigma in their respective organizations. During his career, he has trained and mentored more than 120 Lean Six Sigma Green Belts and Black Belts globally.

Shahbaz has authored more than 40 strategy reports on product development and operational efficiency. He has received professional education in transactional lean methodology, CAP, import/export practices, and GE's leadership essentials. He holds an MBA from Rensselaer Polytechnic Institute, a master's in public policy from the University at Albany, State University of New York, and BAs in French literature and Middle Eastern history from the College at Oneonta, State University of New York. He is Six Sigma Green Belt, BlackBelt, and Master Black Belt certified.